PATCHWORK OF PURPOSE

Crafting a Lasting Legacy through Daily Choices — and — Divine Guidance

TRILOGY
A WHOLLY OWNED SUBSIDIARY OF TBN
PROFESSIONAL PUBLISHING MEETS POWERFUL PROMOTION

TRILOGY
A WHOLLY OWNED SUBSIDIARY OF TBN
PROFESSIONAL PUBLISHING MEETS POWERFUL PROMOTION

Trilogy Christian Publishers
A Wholly Owned Subsidiary of Trinity Broadcasting Network
2442 Michelle Drive
Tustin, CA 92780
Copyright © 2024 by Tessica Davis
All Scripture quotations, unless otherwise noted, taken from THE HOLY BIBLE, NEW INTERNATIONAL VERSION®, NIV® Copyright © 1973, 1978, 1984, 2011 by Biblica, Inc.® Used by permission. All rights reserved worldwide.
All rights reserved, including the right to reproduce this book or portions thereof in any form whatsoever.
For information, address Trilogy Christian Publishing
Rights Department, 2442 Michelle Drive, Tustin, CA 92780.
Trilogy Christian Publishing/ TBN and colophon are trademarks of Trinity Broadcasting Network.
For information about special discounts for bulk purchases, please contact Trilogy Christian Publishing.

Trilogy Disclaimer: The views and content expressed in this book are those of the author and may not necessarily reflect the views and doctrine of Trilogy Christian Publishing or the Trinity Broadcasting Network.

10 9 8 7 6 5 4 3 2 1
Library of Congress Cataloging-in-Publication Data is available.
ISBN 979-8-89333-882-9
ISBN 979-8-89333-883-6 (ebook)

PATCHWORK OF PURPOSE

Crafting a Lasting Legacy through Daily Choices — and — Divine Guidance

TESSICA DAVIS

Dedication

This book is dedicated to the memory of my mother, Valerie Hutchison.

Thank you, Mom, for embodying the spirit of Christ in your life. I hope this book adds to the continuation (in my life) of the legacy you left behind. God reminded me of when you spent hours hand-stitching quilts, drawing a beautiful parallel between the quilt and our lives. May both bring warmth and love to those we leave behind. I wish you were here to share this journey, but I know we will one day be reunited in the presence of our Lord and Savior, Jesus Christ. I love you and miss you every day.

About the Author

Tessica Davis, an author known for her insightful perspectives and transformative storytelling, emerged from the cocoon of a small town to spread her wings across the literary landscape. Born and raised in the charming confines of a close-knit community, Tessica's journey is one of triumph over the confines of small-town thinking, a journey that has ultimately led her to craft this thought-provoking book.

Growing up in a place where tradition and familiarity often intertwined, Tessica found herself drawn to the allure of the unknown from an early age. The limitations of her surroundings ignited a burning desire within her to explore beyond the horizons that her upbringing might have dictated. It was this very struggle against the confinement of narrow perspectives that propelled her to transcend the boundaries that others might have accepted unquestioningly.

Tessica's path was never easy. She encountered skepticism and resistance as she embarked on her quest for knowledge and self-discovery. Yet, she persevered, fueled by a hunger for understanding and an unwavering belief that there was more to life than the familiar contours of her upbringing. Her journey of personal growth led her to confront her own biases, challenge her assumptions, and embrace the diversity of ideas that the world had to offer.

It is from this crucible of experience that Tessica Davis brings you her groundbreaking book, a testament to her resilience and her commitment to unshackling the mind from the constraints of provincial thinking. With each word penned, she extends an invitation to readers to join her in the pursuit of enlightenment, to venture beyond the familiar, and to embrace the vastness of the intellectual and emotional landscape that lies beyond the boundaries of a small town.

Tessica's writing is marked by a unique blend of introspection and expansiveness. Through her words, she imparts the wisdom she gained from her journey of breaking free from the chains of limited perspectives. Her prose is both lyrical and poignant, resonating deeply with those who have ever questioned the boundaries set by their surroundings.

As you delve into Tessica Davis's book, you embark on a journey alongside her—one that leads to growth, understanding, and the liberation of thought. Her narrative is a testament to the power of transformation, reminding us all that with determination and an open mind, we can rise above the limitations that threaten to keep us confined.

Tessica Davis's story is a testament to the fact that the human spirit is capable of soaring to great heights when unburdened by small-town thinking. Through her work, she urges us all to embrace the boundless possibilities that await beyond the horizon and to celebrate the beauty of embracing a world of ideas that knows no borders.

Table of Contents

Dedication	5
About the Author	7
Table of Contents	9
Introduction	13
CHAPTER 1 Stitching the Legacy: Unraveling Life's Quilt	17
CHAPTER 2 Threads of Destiny: Weaving Our Legacy through Life's Choices	23
CHAPTER 3 Embracing Change: Finding Hope in Unexpected Circumstances	29
CHAPTER 4 The Quilt of Understanding: Stitching Empathy in the Patchwork of Humanity	35

CHAPTER 5
Threads of Resilience: Stitching Family
Bonds through Trials and Choices 43

CHAPTER 6
Threads of Reconciliation: Stitching Together
the Legacy of Love 53

CHAPTER 7
Divine Encounters: Finding Purpose in
Unexpected Moments.. 61

CHAPTER 8
Patterns of Purpose: Building Your
Spiritual Tapestry 69

CHAPTER 9
Comfortable Conversations: Building
Uplifting Relationships 79

CHAPTER 10
The Whisper of God: Finding Intimacy
in His Presence 87

CHAPTER 11
Brennan's Legacy: A Journey of Impact
and Inspiration 93

CHAPTER 12
Living Testimonies: Sharing God's Love
through Our Lives.. 103

CHAPTER 13
Breath of Life: Finding Meaning in
Every Exhale 109

CHAPTER 14
Finding Purpose in Life's Mess: Embracing
Authenticity and Compassion 117

CHAPTER 15
Shining Light: Spreading Joy and Love
in Everyday Moments 127

Conclusion: Threads of Legacy 136

Words Of Encouragement from the Author.............. 139

Special Thanks 141

Introduction

The importance of a legacy lies in its ability to leave a lasting impact, shape the future, and contribute to the collective memory of individuals, communities, and society as a whole. Here are some reasons why a legacy is considered significant:

1. **Preserving History and Culture**: Legacies help preserve the history, culture, and values of a particular individual, group, or society. They provide insights into how people lived, thought, and interacted during different periods of time, allowing future generations to learn from the past.

2. **Inspiration and Role Models**: Legacies of remarkable individuals can serve as inspiration and role models for others. People often look up to figures who have achieved great things, overcome challenges, and left a positive mark on the world. These legacies can motivate individuals to pursue their passions, strive for excellence, and make a difference.

3. **Continuity of Knowledge and Ideas**: Intangible legacies, such as ideas, philosophies, and scientific discoveries, can continue to influence intellectual and cultural discourse long after their originators are

gone. This continuity of knowledge contributes to the advancement of fields like science, philosophy, and the arts.

4. **Building a Sense of Identity**: Legacies contribute to the sense of identity and belonging for individuals and communities. They remind people of their roots, traditions, and shared history, fostering a sense of unity and connection among different generations.

5. **Creating Positive Change**: Positive legacies often result from efforts to improve society, address social issues, or advocate for change. These legacies can lead to shifts in attitudes, policies, and behaviors that improve the lives of many.

6. **Passing Down Wisdom**: Personal legacies can include life lessons, experiences, and wisdom gained over a lifetime. By sharing these insights with younger generations, individuals can help others navigate challenges and make more informed decisions.

7. **Contributing to Art and Culture**: Creators leave behind artistic and cultural legacies through their works of art, literature, music, and other creative endeavors. These contributions enrich cultural diversity and provide sources of enjoyment and reflection for people across time.

8. **Fostering Innovation**: The legacies of innovators and inventors can inspire future generations to build upon existing ideas, pushing the boundaries of human knowledge and technology. This progression can lead to new breakthroughs and advancements.

9. **Remembering and Honoring**: Legacies serve as a way to remember and honor the achievements, sacrifices, and contributions of those who came before us. This recognition ensures that their efforts are not forgotten and that their impact continues to be acknowledged.

In essence, legacies have the power to transcend time, leaving a mark that extends far beyond an individual's or group's existence. They provide a means for people to connect with the past, envision the future, and contribute positively to the ongoing story of humanity.

The concept of legacy is multifaceted and can apply to various aspects of life, culture, history, and technology. It's often about what is left behind and how it continues to shape the world beyond its initial creation or use.

"For I know the plans I have for you, declares the Lord, plans for welfare and not for evil, to give you a future and a hope."
— Jeremiah 29:11

— CHAPTER 1 —
Stitching the Legacy: Unraveling Life's Quilt

When I started writing this book I wanted to share our family legacy, so I began to think about my mom and how she would spend hours and hours, day after day quilting by hand. After about a four-year battle with cancer, she passed away at the age of thirty-three. Us four kids' ranged from 10 to 15 years-of-age. My father had a lot to deal with. I have very few memories that I can recall of my mother, so you can only imagine why this one is so special to me. No matter how big the crowd is, I love to tell this story. If I am sharing one-on-one, in a small intimate group, or to a room full of people, I love to tell this story. This is my story, my lessons, my struggles, and some of my victories. This is what God used to shape me into who He wanted me to become. I hope this will help you in your struggles, help you rejoice in your victories, and help you to begin to think about what legacy you will leave behind. Will your legacy be positive? Will it help future generations? Will your thoughts and accomplishments bring joy to those who remember you? Will your legacy inspire others?

— PATCHWORK OF PURPOSE —

My mother's name is Valerie. She was a very loving person. She was well-liked everywhere she went. She enjoyed hunting and spending time outdoors, but mostly she enjoyed being with her family, helping us in every way. She would sew a lot of our clothes and even quilted the blankets we used in the winter. She had a sewing machine to make our clothes. However, with the blankets, every stitch of the quilting was made by her hand. She would sit for hours, days, and weeks stitching. What was the purpose? The purpose was to create something that would keep her family warm in the winter.

The house I grew up in did not have central heat or air. In the winter, our bedrooms would get very cold. Well, cold to us. In Southeast Texas, the cold here is different than if we were in the north, but we did have some winters where snow stuck to the ground. Our house was a work in progress. Unfinished walls, metal roof that dripped condensation from the roofing nails when it sweat, and no ceiling separating the room from the roof except for in the living room and kitchen. The floors were made up of 2x6 boards that allowed us to see the ground under the floor when the light would shine just right. Our wood-burning stoves in the living room and kitchen were our only source of heat except for a very small electric heater for the sectioned-off bathing area of the restroom. As you can see, it was a very humble house. My father promised my mother that he would build her a house and he was going to do it by hand. As the family grew, we had to move into the house before it was complete, therefore the conditions were not ideal. After she became ill, all construction on the house stopped, and the focus was on her and her health. Despite her illness, my mother continued to sew the majority of our clothes and make our blankets by quilting.

— TESSICA DAVIS —

Some of my fondest memories are of watching my mom work on the quilts. She would never complain. She enjoyed what she was doing and knowing it would benefit her family made the task even more special to her. She would allow me to sit with her as she explained how and what she was doing. She even let me help her from time to time. It was a very special moment for me. I would see her from time to time sit back in her chair, rub her hands, and stretch her back as if they were hurting. I am sure they were after hand-stitching for hours. She would rest only for a moment and then resume her work. Over the years she made several different styles and sizes of quilts. Have you ever crafted anything by hand? Do you think it is possible to sum up your life's work in one project?

The quilt/project we are going to talk about is what we call the scrap quilt. The reason we call this one a scrap quilt is because it was made up of just that. My mother would save scrap materials, leftovers from other projects, or fabrics she would find on clearance marked down to 10 cents a yard. Every piece of fabric had its own story. This one was from a dress she made for me, that one was from a shirt she made my dad, another would be left over from a pair of shorts she made my sister, each piece came from somewhere different. She would carefully measure them out, cut them into triangles, and sew them together. She would begin with two random pieces and sew them together to make a square and then set it aside. She would then grab two other pieces and sew them together to make a square. She would continue this process for a long time until she felt like she had enough to start to combine. She would then proceed to take one square and sew it to another and another. Four small squares made a larger square. After she had four of the larger squares, she would stitch them together

— PATCHWORK OF PURPOSE —

to make yet an even larger square. She would measure the bed that this specific quilt was intended for, so she knew the exact measurements she needed for the quilt to cover the bed. After she had the squares, all measured out, lined up, and stitched together, the fun part started. Wouldn't it be amazing if you could measure out the memories you will leave behind? I can assure you that it is possible.

Like I said, now the fun part starts. She would then find the backing material for the back side of the quilt and put it into the quilting frames, line it with cotton, and then place the top layer she created from the scraps on top. She would bolt down the wooden quilting frames on all sides, roll them in as far as she could, and start quilting. She would always start from the inside and work her way to the edges. One stitch at a time. The purpose of the stitching is to bind together the scrap layer on top, the cotton center, and the solid piece on the bottom. She would always begin from the center so the final project would be smooth, without bulging or missed areas. If any area of the quilt was not stitched together it would not hold through the test of time. The loose cotton in the center would ball up and cause the quilt to start coming apart after a few times through the washing machine. She wanted to make sure that this quilt would outlast rambunctious kids and the pounding of the washer and dryer.

She would spend countless hours stitching these layers together. After each section, she would roll out another area of the frames to give her a new working space. Once all areas were quilted, she would then fold the edges and stitch them closed to complete the project. It was always a happy day when she would complete one of her quilts. They were made up of a variety of colors and textures. They were beautiful and very much appreciated.

Now that you have a quick understanding of how to create a quilt, let me explain why I took you through all that. I look at this scrap quilt and think it is a lot like life. As we go through our daily lives, we create our own patterns or pieces of fabric. Today was a good day, my fabric that represents today is bright and bold, or today was mediocre and my fabric is gray with little yellow polka dots on it. Some days are rougher than others and maybe this pattern looks more like an array of dingy stripes. No matter what the fabric of today looks like it will be measured and cut into a triangle to be used in one of the smaller squares.

Every day of our lives we create a pattern. Each pattern is stitched together to create our life quilt. The quilt is later used to warm our family in our absence. When we are no longer a part of this earth, the memory of who we are remains. The differences we made. The challenges we faced. Our mistakes, and our victories, all play a part in who we are and the legacy we leave behind.

As God stitches our pieces together, He starts from the middle or inside. As He continues, will He like what He sees? Will your family be proud of what they see and feel? It is never too late to start making changes. We all have areas we need to improve. Some of the changes may be outward where others can see them and some of them may be inward where only you and God can see.

What pattern will you create today? Tomorrow? And in the days to come?

As you continue with the following chapters, I will share some real-life stories and share with you how this can help you look at situations differently and take steps to improve your very own life quilt. The Bible says over and over to renew your mind, meaning to look at situations differently, react differently, and know that God is here with you no matter what your situation looks like. Please continue and take this journey with me and start thinking of what legacy you will leave behind.

In reflecting on my mother's perseverance and dedication to crafting quilts, I am reminded of a verse from Colossians 3:23-24: "Whatever you do, work at it with all your heart, as working for the Lord, not for human masters, since you know that you will receive an inheritance from the Lord as a reward. It is the Lord Christ you are serving." Just as my mother poured her heart into every stitch, may we too approach our tasks with such dedication, knowing that our efforts are ultimately serving a greater purpose in God's eyes.

Furthermore, when considering the intricate process of piecing together scraps of fabric to create something beautiful, I am reminded of Jeremiah 29:11: "For I know the plans I have for you, declares the Lord, plans for welfare and not for evil, to give you a future and a hope." Just as each scrap found purpose in my mother's quilt, may we trust that every piece of our lives, even the seemingly insignificant ones, contributes to God's greater plan for us.

As we reflect on the legacy we leave behind, may we heed the words of Proverbs 22:1: "A good name is to be chosen rather than great riches, and favor is better than silver or gold." Let us strive to leave behind a legacy of love, faithfulness, and service to others, knowing that these are the true treasures in life.

Now, let us continue on this journey of self-reflection and growth, as we explore the lessons embedded within the threads of our lives, guided by the wisdom of scripture and the example set by those who have gone before us.

CHAPTER 2
Threads of Destiny: Weaving Our Legacy through Life's Choices

As we delve into the intricate fabric of life's choices and their consequences, it's essential to ground ourselves in biblical wisdom. Life presents us with myriad situations, some of which may seem daunting or overwhelming. However, it's crucial to discern between mere situations and genuine problems. Challenges like the loss of a job, familial concerns, or unexpected turns can test our resolve and faith. Yet, as we navigate these circumstances, we must remember the words of James 1:2-3, encouraging us to find joy amidst trials. Our responses to these situations shape the fabric of our lives, determining whether they become burdens or opportunities for growth.

When you are confronted with something unexpected, how do you handle it? Have you ever wondered why you have situations in your life? Almost every day I hear people complain about, "I have this 'problem,' or "I have that 'problem,' when it is not a problem at all. These are situa-

— PATCHWORK OF PURPOSE —

tions. Loss of a job, a situation. Special needs child, a situation. A child with an illness, a situation. A broken-down vehicle, family concerns, rough childhood, absent parent, abuse, infidelity, unexpected grandchild, bills to pay, these are all situations. Now, how we handle these situations will determine if it turns into a problem or an opportunity. In the following chapters, we will cover many of these situations and how they may or may not turn into problems and examine each day to find out what type of fabric is added to your personal life quilt.

> *"Consider it pure joy, my brothers and sisters,*
> *whenever you face trials of many kinds,*
> *because you know that the testing of*
> *your faith produces perseverance."*
> — *James 1:2-3*

I am a firm believer that your day and your situations are what you make of them. When unexpected things come up, it is important to think about how we will respond to them. Each day when we choose to get out of bed—and yes, it is a choice—it is up to us as individuals to make the best of the situation we are currently in. The reason I say "currently in" is because the situation can always change. When most people hear you say that they automatically think the worst things possible, but what if this one turns for the better today? A lot of the results we find are based on the effort we put in. That's not to say you can be doing everything you know to do to improve the situation and every day it seems to stay the same. Have you done more research? Have you asked for help? Have you prayed specifically for this situation?

— TESSICA DAVIS —

*"Commit to the Lord whatever you do,
and He will establish your plans."*
— Proverbs 16:3

Sometimes I was left in a situation until I decided to make a change of my own. Maybe I needed to improve my attitude and that person that pushes my button every single day is put in my life to help me learn that lesson. Maybe I lost that job because I was putting it in front of my family or God. Sometimes what we choose to sacrifice is not always in our best interest. Yes, you lost that large income, but you gained time with your family. Use it wisely, there is always another job out there. Do not ever think your current employment has to be your last.

*"Trust in the Lord with all your heart
and lean not on your own understanding;
in all your ways submit to Him, and
He will make your paths straight."*
— Proverbs 3:5-6

What about that two-hour road trip both ways (with weather and traffic it could take three) to get to the hospital and the visit is only one hour and forty-five minutes. You make the trip two times a week. You see the worry, the stress, all that fuel, all that time in the car, the extra money spent because you stop for fuel or bathroom breaks and buy snacks and treats at your favorite fuel station. Is this a problem? No, but it is a situation that I have found myself in recently. Did I really accomplish anything? Why is this trip necessary week after week? There are lots of situations we find ourselves in that should make us question things, but instead, we only complain. We do not look for a solution.

— PATCHWORK OF PURPOSE —

"And we know that in all things God works for the good of those who love Him, who have been called according to His purpose."
— Romans 8:28

Over the years I have been introduced to several different types of training. Basic education training, biblical training, inspiration, motivation, and others. The best training I feel I have is life. God uses life training to teach us how to deal with our situations. No book can tell me how to feel, no teacher can show me how to process this new feeling or information. At least, none that I have found. Now, with that being said, there is a lot of information out there that is helpful to the situation, but the ultimate decision to respond, react, or just except is a personal one. Truth be told, that is the thing that matters the most in any situation. Do you react? For the longest time, I was a reactor. I would fly off the handle in a millisecond. I would allow the situation to affect my whole day. I have learned responding and reacting are two totally different things. In any situation, YOU choose the ending. God will guide you and show you the way, but the choice is yours.

"A person's steps are directed by the Lord. How then can anyone understand their own way?"
— Proverbs 20:24

Do you remember those books we read when we were in grade school? The adventure books where the ending is based on your choice. "If you choose option A turn to page 12, if you choose option B turn to page 187." You can read that same book five or six times and get a different outcome based on your choice. The story advances based on you.

TESSICA DAVIS

You decide the twists and turns. Well, our day-to-day life is the same way. I can choose option A or option B in every situation I find myself in. I remember I picked up one of these books and started reading. For the first choice, I chose wrong. After making my choice and turning to the appropriate page the main character died and the book was over. I just closed the book thinking, "What a waste!" but was it? I remembered the first choice I made, it was option B. I reopened the book and started over and when I got to the first choice again, I chose option A. Guess what happened then? The story continued. My point in all that is that it is okay to relive a situation if it helps you get to a different path. Do not always make the choice others think you will or should. Be you. Make the best decision for you and your family. Seek God and His will for you. Learn from the past; you may be choosing the options that keep you where you are. God has a plan for your life. Ask Him to show you the path you should be taking.

> *"Your word is a lamp for my feet, a light on my path."*
> — Psalm 119:105

If ever you find yourself in a situation where you made the wrong choice, the best thing I can share with you is a congratulations. Even though it may have caused you pain, you have educated yourself in these situations and guess what? You can now make a better choice. Take responsibility. Pick yourself up, dust yourself off, and keep going. It will be a little difficult at times. Others may have to forgive you if your choice affected them negatively. Some people may exit your life. Some will take longer to come around than others. It is going to take time but know that every step is worth it.

— PATCHWORK OF PURPOSE —

You can do it. You have the strength you do not know you have. God's word says, "I can do all things through Christ who strengthens me" (Philippians 4:13). Believe in yourself. Every step in the correct direction is a victory. Congratulate yourself.

> *"And we know that in all things God works for the good of those who love Him, who have been called according to His purpose."*
> *— Romans 8:28*

As we reflect on the lessons embedded within the threads of our lives, guided by the wisdom of scripture and the examples set by those who have gone before us, it becomes evident that our choices shape not only our present but also our legacy. In the fabric of life, each decision we make adds a thread, contributing to the intricate pattern of our existence. But as we navigate the twists and turns of life's journey, we must also acknowledge the inevitability of change.

As we reflect on the consequences of our decisions and the paths they pave, we must also acknowledge the inevitability of change. Just as every quilt undergoes transformation with each added stitch, so do our lives evolve amidst unexpected circumstances. Join me in the next chapter as we explore the transformative power of embracing change and finding hope amidst life's twists and turns.

CHAPTER 3
Embracing Change: Finding Hope in Unexpected Circumstances

As we confront the theme of embracing change and finding hope in unexpected circumstances, it's vital to draw upon the wisdom of scripture. Life often throws curveballs, challenging our routines and expectations. The loss of a job, for example, can disrupt our sense of stability and our feeling of purpose. However, amidst these trials, we're reminded of the promise in Romans 8:28, that God works all things for the good of those who love Him. Even in the face of uncertainty, we're encouraged to trust in His plan and seek opportunities for growth and renewal. Let's journey together through the chapters ahead, exploring the transformative power of faith and resilience in navigating life's twists and turns.

As many of us know, the loss of a job can be devastating. What is the devastating part? Is it the loss of the J O B or is it the loss of the income, status, self-worth, or sense of belonging? As we get up each day most of us are like robots.

— PATCHWORK OF PURPOSE —

My alarm goes off at the same time every morning. If I get out of the door on time, I see the same vehicles on the road. I take the same route to work, and I have noticed that the same white truck flies past me around the same place on the road each day. I started looking for him (I assume it is a man and he is on his way to the plant up the road. He must make it on time or the entry will be locked.) As I stop at the same fast-food drive-in for my 44oz sweet tea I notice the same minivan, car, and SUV. We all have our routines we get into. Add any change in this and we feel lost.

With the loss of a job, now your routine is shattered. No four a.m. alarm. No reason to rush out the door. Now it would require a special trip to get your favorite morning beverage. No one is expecting to see you today. No expectation of seeing those you were around every day for many years. The feeling of being lost. *What am I supposed to accomplish today? How am I supposed to support my family, pay the bills, and continue with my lifestyle? What will the neighbors think to see my vehicle in the drive all day today?* Imagine the stress this will put on someone. Has it happened to you or someone you know? Can you relate? Are you in this situation now? Even now as I sit here and type my anxiety is starting to rise just thinking of all the negative emotions.

Let us change direction, shall we? Take a deep breath. Do not let yourself be down because of this. Get up and drink coffee with your spouse in the mornings. Take the children to school and kiss them on the head before they go about their day. Go have lunch with your mom, dad, or another family member you have not seen in a while. Stop and take a walk in the park. Take time to reboot. I know some of you are probably thinking, *This is not going to pay the bills* or *This will not help my situation.* You never know what will happen, whom you will meet, or what opportunities are waiting for you.

— TESSICA DAVIS —

During the time I was out on FMLA for a much-needed surgery, my family situation changed dramatically. I went from not thinking I would ever be a grandparent one minute, to news that my daughter is pregnant, to the baby being here three weeks later. My daughter was having some complications and was put on hospital bed rest. I was able to spend two days with her before I was admitted to a different hospital in a different city for my surgery. Some people would look at this as a problem. We see it as a situation. What are we going to do about it? How are we going to make this work? I felt the need to be with her but was unable to do so. My daughter's situation got much more serious, and we were trying to work with the hospital (during the COVID pandemic of 2020) for someone to be with her until I could travel. They told us I was the only one who could visit except for her husband. He was unable to stay with her because of his work schedule and the hospital she was in was too far to drive every day after work for him. If he went to see her, he would not make it to work.

I was unable to travel after my surgery so we were trying to figure out how we could make sure my daughter wasn't left in a strange city, laying in a hospital bed all alone during the COVID pandemic. After getting permission from the hospital, my sister (having a day off work due to the weather) decided to make the two-hour drive to the hospital for the day. After watching my daughter for several hours my sister was convinced my daughter was in labor even though the machines were not picking up any contractions. Long story short, my daughter was rushed in for an emergency cesarean section delivery. At twenty weeks, she delivered a 1lb 3oz micro-preemie little boy. At this point, we were all uncertain as to what came next. Knowing my daughter and my new grandson would need my help after her surgery and with him needing an extended stay in the NICU, my husband and I decided it would be best that I did not return to my regular job after my recovery. This was a very hard decision. Loss of income, loss of daily routine, and loss of feeling needed all took over. The answer came to me as fast as the negative thoughts. My daughter was able to stay with us while she recovered. Her husband works crazy shift work, and she would have been left by herself for long hours at a time. With all her restrictions, this was the best answer we could come up with. From driving her back to the hospital (two hours away) to visit the baby a few times a week, to taking her to her doctor appointments along with my follow-up appointments, my schedule was very full.

I found myself awake very early one morning with all these clear images in my head. I picked up a pen and started writing. After an extended time of getting my web page set up, I started a blog and began to write this book. I later decided to stop the blog and concentrate my energy here.

With this new direction, I found myself excited about all its possibilities. I knew I had been working in a field I did not enjoy. Twelve-hour days and working weekends in a field that did not interest me was very hard. I am a true believer in the phrase, "if you do a job, do it well," which had been pounded in me for years. I put my best foot forward and I was very good at what I did. After speaking with my boss, we all decided it was okay and I was able to leave with a good recommendation. I think it is important to preserve relationships when you can and leave any position on good terms if at all possible. Now I can spend more time with my family, giving them the help they need while doing something I truly love to do.

When my family and I decided that I would not return to my current job, we knew it would be difficult financially.

As we proceed month to month and day to day we just keep pushing forward. God's word says, "But my God shall supply all your need according to His riches in glory by Christ Jesus" (Philippians 4:19). I believe this was my true calling and if I stay in God's will and in my true calling, He will supply all that is needed for all the other stuff to fall in line. And that is exactly what has happened. I am not saying everything came easy, sometimes we had to just wait and trust that God would provide, and He did. I had to give up a few things to make it work, but they were not life-threatening and in the grand scheme of things they did not matter as much as I thought at the time.

If you find yourself in the "loss of job" situation please remember, you were looking for a job when you found that one. There will be something out there for you. You may even find yourself doing something you love versus doing something just for the paycheck. Take a walk. Clear your mind. Get inspired. Start thinking about what it was you wanted to do when you were younger. Is that still a realistic career? If so, I encourage you to chase that rain cloud. You can do it! Show the next generation you can start over in your career and everything will still work out okay. You do not have to stay in the rut you find yourself in today. That everyday routine may not be what God intended for you. God's word says, "I know the plans I have for you, plans to prosper you and not to harm you, plans to give you hope and a future" (Jeremiah 29:11). He may have a much bigger plan. Find it. Chase it. Ask God to reveal the path He has for you.

1. **Psalm 34:17-18**—"The righteous cry out, and the Lord hears them; He delivers them from all their troubles. The Lord is close to the brokenhearted and saves those who are crushed in spirit."

PATCHWORK OF PURPOSE

2. **Isaiah 41:10**—"So do not fear, for I am with you; do not be dismayed, for I am your God. I will strengthen you and help you; I will uphold you with my righteous right hand."

3. **Romans 8:28**—"And we know that in all things God works for the good of those who love Him, who have been called according to His purpose."

4. **Matthew 6:25-26**—"Therefore I tell you, do not worry about your life, what you will eat or drink; or about your body, what you will wear. Is not life more than food, and the body more than clothes? Look at the birds of the air; they do not sow or reap or store away in barns, and yet your heavenly Father feeds them. Are you not much more valuable than they?"

As we journey through the intricacies of life, we encounter moments that challenge our perceptions and broaden our understanding of humanity. Just as every stitch in a quilt contributes to its beauty, so too do our interactions with others shape the fabric of our society. Now, as we turn the page to the next chapter, let us delve deeper into the quilt of understanding, where the threads of compassion weave a tapestry of connection across diverse experiences and perspectives.

— CHAPTER 4 —
The Quilt of Understanding: Stitching Empathy in the Patchwork of Humanity

Today, the term "special needs child" is very common. It touches almost every family in America in one way or another. If one of your family members does not hold the title, you most likely know someone who does. There are many different reasons why a person would be considered special needs. Is it hearing, speaking, walking, breathing, eating, or the way they think and learn? Yes, I know I just referred to that special child as a person, because that is what they are.

We as adults get all tied up in the whole idea of what it takes to be "an adult." You must have a job. You must hold a title. You must have your car. You must own your home. There are different things we put on ourselves that some people will never be able to accomplish, but that does not mean they are any less of a person than you are.

Have you ever been in a public place and heard a child screaming at the top of his lungs? Did you immediately judge the parent? Most of the time, and I am as guilty as

— PATCHWORK OF PURPOSE —

anyone else, we think badly of the parent. After all, discipline is the parent's responsibility. What if what you think you hear and see is altogether different? What if that is the scream of a child who is trying to communicate and does not have the ability to do so at the time? What if this is the only thing he or she knows? What if it is a sensory issue and they are having a meltdown because they don't understand yet how to maneuver in this situation? What if the parent HAS done everything correctly and the child is just having a bad day? If you have never spent time with a child who cannot communicate, think of it like this: What if you were a young adult and for whatever reason you lost the ability to speak? You cannot put two words together to save your life or those around you. How would you tell the person next to you that the house is on fire? I know with all the technology in the world you would text or write a note or even email. What if those options are not there for you? What would you do? You would scream. This child is trying to communicate with his/her parent and does not have the means to do so. The only thing they can do is scream until the parent figures out what they are trying to communicate. This child is so cut off from this world and it is our job to figure out how to reach them. At the time, you may not think the situation is all that bad, but you do not live inside their head. You have no idea what it is they are dealing with. What might be meaningless to you could be devastating to them. Please, I beg you, do not judge the parents, and do not judge the child.

    I have the privilege to know a few special children. They can be very entertaining when they want to be. They are like any other child. They need love. They need understanding. They need us to find a way to reach them. I have a story to tell you about a little girl I know. Her name is Laura and I have permission from her family to tell you about her. Laura is a young girl who does not speak much. She listens. She understands, but she does not respond very often. I spent time with her mother and would be with her when she picked Laura up from school from time to time. Laura would get in the SUV and climb in her car seat. She knew that was where she had to sit in the car without being reminded. I would look at her and say, "Hello, Laura. How was your day?" Knowing I would not get a response I would follow it up with a complement. Either telling her I liked her shoes or her shirt, or just simply telling her she is pretty. My friend would just strap Laura in, and we would continue with the other stops we had to make. Most days we would leave Laura's school and drive across town to pick up the rest of my friends' kids. Our town has five different school campuses.

One day we picked up Laura like normal and then had to pick up my son Brock from work because his truck was in the shop. Now keep in mind Laura was in first or second grade and Brock had already graduated high school. I will tell you all about Brock in a minute but just know Brock is special in his own way. As Brock entered the vehicle, he looked at Laura and said hello like always. We proceeded to head to the nearest drive-through so we could get half-price drinks because it was still happy hour, and I would love a sweet tea right about then. Laura gets a red slushie and Brock gets a blue coconut slushie. Just a few minutes down the road Laura starts busting out laughing. We were concerned at first because she did not show this much emotion very often. My friend and I were trying to figure out what had her so worked up and why she was laughing so hard. Thinking she was going to spill this red drink all over the carpet of the SUV, I turned around to see what was going on in the back seat. Laura was laughing at Brock because his tongue was now blue. He stuck his tongue out and she just lost it. She was laughing so hard she had tears in her eyes. Can you imagine how just this little thing opened her up? We continued this same routine a few days in a row; we would get Laura from school and then go get Brock, One day, as Brock entered the vehicle, he greeted Laura like he always did. Laura said, "Hello, Brock." Clear as day. There was no mistake that she knew exactly who he was. Her mother and I were floored. We did not even know she knew his name because she had never even tried to say it before. As many times as I had greeted Laura, she had never spoken to me but she bolted out a very clear and loud, "Hello, Brock." It was such a proud moment for us all. I was happy to see her connect with someone.

The same school year, we noticed that Laura would scream and point each time we passed the same intersection as we drove across town. She would scream out "washasheen, washasheen." Not knowing what she meant by this, one day we decided to turn around and see what she was trying to tell us. We had a few minutes to spare and wanted to investigate. After turning around and taking a right at the intersection, we passed a car wash and she pointed and yelled out "washasheen, washasheen". I told my friend as we were both laughing that she wanted to go to the car wash. We turned around again and took her through the automatic car wash. Laura got so excited she was kicking her feet and swinging her arms like crazy. I had never seen her show so much emotion. As the days went on, each time (and it was not every day) she would scream "washasheen" we would go to the car wash. It only took a few extra minutes of our time, and it gave her such joy to watch the bubbles roll down the windows and hear the spray of the water hit the vehicle. Each time we went we would tell her, "Laura, say car wash." After a few weeks Laura said, "Car wash." It was such a small thing but at the same time, it was a large victory for Laura. If we had not taken the extra time, we would have prevented Laura's victory. We could have just told her to stop screaming and be quiet, but had we done that, she would not have had this breakthrough.

Keep in mind, all breakthroughs and victories do not have to be on a grand scale. Sometimes it is the little victories that give us the push we need to keep going. We can make a difference in the lives of those around us. All we need to do is keep our eyes and ears open and the possibilities will present themselves.

I mentioned earlier that I would tell you about Brock, so here is a little about him. In his earlier days he would go to school and do the best he could do, but he had a hard time focusing on his work. He would spend all day at school and bring home a lot of homework every day. We would spend four or more hours at the kitchen table trying to finish his work. When he was in the third grade, I could not figure out why he had so much more homework than the other kids. After talking to his teacher, I found out that Brock would not finish his classroom assignments so she would send them home. After months of this struggle, and it was a struggle to help him stay focused, we had a breakthrough. We were preparing to attend church as it was a Wednesday, I packed up his schoolwork to bring with us. Brock liked to attend the children's church on Wednesdays. Knowing we were going to be up late to finish his work, I kept Brock in "big church" with me. We always start the service with praise and worship. I had communicated with Brock that he was going to sit next to me and work on his schoolwork. If he finished, he would be allowed to join his friends in kids' service. He had a math worksheet that he needed to complete. Normally I would have to point to each math problem

— PATCHWORK OF PURPOSE —

before he would try to solve it. As the music started, I stood and engaged in worship after instructing Bock to remain seated and work on his math. After the second song, I sat down to help Brock focus and continue with his worksheet. As I sat down, I was astonished at what I was looking at. Brock sat there with a big smile on his face and the entire worksheet was completed. Any other time, this would have taken us an hour or so to complete. My immediate thought was what better place for a miracle than sitting in church? After letting him run off to be with his friends I began to think. Was it a miracle? Did God just use this circumstance to teach me something? The music helped him stay focused. Over the next few weeks, I would play praise and worship music while we did his homework, and you know what? IT WORKED. We were able to finish his work much faster. The one thing I have learned is, we as parents and adults must learn how to enter the child's world. This earth is a big scary place and they do not always know how to communicate or participate in our world. In raising Brock and spending time with Laura this lesson became very clear to me.

How is this relatable if we are not talking about a special needs person? Well, my answer is: Are we all not special needs people? We may not have the medical difficulties others have. We may not have speech delay. We may not have trouble walking, learning, or understanding, but is there something in our life that we are hoping others understand? Maybe it is the way you speak or walk. Maybe it is the way you learn. Maybe it is the way you drive (yes, I raised my hand on that one). Maybe it is the way you care. Maybe it is the way you express love. We are all different. We are all special in our own way. God created us all differently. Please, I ask you, look around. Who in your life needs a little extra understanding? Who needs an extra hand with a project?

— TESSICA DAVIS —

Who needs someone to just listen? God's word says, "A new commandment I give unto you, That you love one another, as I have loved you" (John 13:34). We all have things about us others do not understand. I have things about myself I do not understand. Open your eyes, open your heart. Be the difference in your circle of influence. Ask the questions and offer help. Stop what you are doing and listen to the people around you. Maybe you will understand them better, maybe they will understand you better. This will grow your influence and increase your impact. Let others see Jesus in you. In doing this, we can create a better legacy we will leave behind. Kindness is catching. Maybe someone will see you being kind and in turn will do some of the same.

1. **Proverbs 31:8-9**—"Speak up for those who cannot speak for themselves, for the rights of all who are destitute. Speak up and judge fairly; defend the rights of the poor and needy."

2. **Matthew 25:40**—"The King will reply, 'Truly I tell you, whatever you did for one of the least of these brothers and sisters of mine, you did for me.'"

3. **Romans 12:10**—"Be devoted to one another in love. Honor one another above yourselves."

4. **Philippians 2:4**—"Not looking to your own interests but each of you to the interests of the others."

5. **Ephesians 4:32**—"Be kind and compassionate to one another, forgiving each other, just as in Christ God forgave you."

As we reflect on the threads of compassion that bind us together in the quilt of understanding, we are reminded of

PATCHWORK OF PURPOSE

the importance of nurturing kindness in our interactions with others. Just as each stitch contributes to the beauty of a quilt, so too do our acts of compassion enrich the fabric of humanity. In the pages to come, let us continue this journey by exploring the significance of cultivating a garden of kindness in the landscape of life.

CHAPTER 5
Threads of Resilience: Stitching Family Bonds through Trials and Choices

The relationship between me and my dad was always a little different. As a young child, I tried to stay out of my dad's way. When he was home, I would try to stay in the other room. I was always a little scared of my dad, mostly because I stayed in a lot of trouble. I was a rambunctious and rebellious child. It is not that I tried to disobey; it just seemed to be the way it was. Almost as if I could not do anything without it being wrong. If I was told not to do something, it was a magnet for me. It seemed like I couldn't stop myself from doing it. I was very determined. Most of the time, it was my mouth and my attitude that would get me into trouble. I would say something he did not like, and so it would begin.

My dad worked a lot of hours and was not home a lot during the daytime hours. Even on the weekends, he was busy with the hunting club, working with the animals, or a variety of other projects around the house. Being the third of four children, I tried to stay invisible. I do not have the memories of sitting in my dad's lap, getting hugs and kisses, or much affection at all from him. I do not remember him being a very affectionate person, although I am sure he had his moments.

When I was in the fourth grade, my mom was diagnosed with cancer and was very sick. Her treatments made her weak and sick to her stomach most of the time. When we were all at home, most of our time was spent cleaning or trying to help take care of my mom. My dad would help as much as he could when he was there, but his work kept him away for long hours at a time.

For as long as I can remember, my dad was on the board of the local hunting lease. Throughout the years we made several trips to the woods. Cleaning campgrounds, making sure roads were clear, checking sign-in sheets, and several other things I am sure I was unaware of. He took his role very seriously. We as a family would sometimes just ride the roads in the lease. My mom loved being in the outdoors. I am sure he was checking on one thing or another, but for us kids, it just seemed like we were riding for the fun of it. I must admit, I enjoyed my time in the woods. It was the few times I did not have anything pressing to do and could just relax. Even then, from time to time, my mouth would get away from me and I would say something to get in trouble. If I could only learn to keep my mouth shut. Well, that is a skill I have yet to learn, but I am still working on it.

As I sit and try to remember, I have only a few repeating memories. I say repeating because it is something that would happen often. Back in the 1980s, before cell phones, we had a rotary phone that hung on the wall. It had a long spiral cord that would stretch from the phone receiver to the base where it hung on the wall. The cord was long enough to stretch from the base that hung on the wall just inside the kitchen to my dad's recliner that sat in the living room. He would say, "Go call Westley and bring me the phone." I would go to the phone, unwind the twisted cord because it was always a knotted mess, and dial Mr. Westley's number. Before bringing the phone to my dad I would make sure someone answered on the other end. I dialed it so much that I can still remember that phone number to this day. Sitting here typing I smile because I could recite it to you, but I will not because the last I heard the number remains operational as Mr. Westley's home number. Yes, I know that is a foreign concept nowadays. Now, this memory is not grand by any means, but it is an example of me interacting with my dad without getting myself into trouble.

    I can recall my dad calling me or one of my siblings out of our rooms to change the channel on the television set. We had the kind of television that had a round knob to change stations. Click, click, channel 4. Then we wait to see if that is something he may want to watch. No. Click, click, channel 6. Waiting again. We only had about four or five channels to choose from, but this could go on for a while. Waiting until the commercials were over just to see what program was playing. And you would know, each time we changed the station there would be another commercial. No remote, no guide to search, no satellite, or cable, we had an antenna and could only get signal from the nearest local stations. I guess the funniest thing was when we had a set of rabbit ears for the antenna, this was before we got the big one outside that would boost us up a few more stations when the weather was good. Most young people nowadays have no idea what I am talking about but that is okay. I encourage you to search it out on the web. You will be amazed that "people actually lived like that," at least that is what I hear from my kids. Back to the rabbit ears. We had aluminum foil, yes, the kind you cook with, wrapped around the ends of the rabbit ears to boost the signal. Depending on the weather we would have to adjust the antenna. Dad would be sitting in his recliner, and I would be standing to the side but just a step behind the television moving the antenna ears. First one way and then another, back and forth until I found the correct setting where the picture was clear. Oh, but do not worry, when he wanted to change the station, the game started all over again. Most of the time he was searching for an old western movie to watch. He did not have a lot of downtime, so when he wanted to watch television, westerns were what we would watch. Back then, unlike now, there was only one television in the house. I must admit, that is not the case in my house presently. Looking back, I am sure it helped with family bonding because we would all sit together. Nowadays, everyone goes their separate ways to watch TV or play games.

Even though those are silly, they are the only memories I have as a child of me and my dad where there was no arguing, no mouthing back, or anything like that. It was simply an unconfrontational exchange. Over the years, my mouth would continue to keep me in trouble, so those rare moments of easy exchange were precious.

The August before I started eighth grade my mom died. Her struggles were finally over. My dad was left with four kids to continue to raise on his own. My Granny and Paw (his mom and dad) lived next door. There was a small pond that separated our place and theirs. My Aunt (dad's sister) lived on the backside of us. We lived on family land that had been divided up between my dad and his siblings. Each family had eight acres, so we had plenty of room to keep us occupied outside. We had family close by if we needed anything. We would often get home from school long before he would arrive home from work, so we started dinner and made sure the house was tidy for his arrival. We were also responsible for the laundry. We basically had to take on all the household responsibilities because when dad got home, it was too late for him to do a lot of things. I did not enjoy having to go to school and then come home and help take care of the animals, the house, the dishes, the yard, etc. I was bitter about it all.

I had anger issues I had to learn to control. After my mom passed the anger issues got worse. I was not a nice person. Sure, I had my share of friends, one or two good ones, who would try to understand me. I blame that on having good Christian parents that encouraged them to be nice to me. Most of the people I would encounter would just try to keep their distance. I had a few adults who would encourage and compliment me, but I was so stubborn, angry, and bitter, I am sure I would just walk away with an ungrateful attitude.

One day I found myself assigned to the front seat on the school bus to and from school. I am sure my mouth got me there. I was rude to almost everyone, kids and adults alike, even my dad. On this particular day, I found myself in a fistfight on the school bus on the ride home from school because something was said and I allowed it to make me even more angry. I let my anger get the best of me and made some pretty bad choices in the heat of the moment. My anger was so bad, it was almost uncontrollable. When I arrived home, it was a strange day because my dad was already there. I am unsure as to why he was home early. Maybe he got rained out, maybe he just decided to take some time off, maybe he had some business to take care of and had to leave work early, I do not know. What I do know is when I saw his truck in the driveway and him standing in the front yard, I just knew

— PATCHWORK OF PURPOSE —

I was going to get the whipping of my life. My brother and my two sisters got off the bus filled with excitement, ready to tell him all about it. As I crossed the street in front of the bus, I just hung my head. Most of the other kids had already been dropped off at their stops; we were the second or third to last stop on the route, so I had plenty of time to make up the scenario in my head as to how this was going to go. As I walked toward my dad, I could hear my younger sister and my brother talking over each other telling my dad all about what had happened. As I slowly walked up to him, he simply looked down and me and asked, "Well, did you win?" My head still hanging I replied, "Yes sir." He asked, "Did you start the fight?" I then explained the events leading up to the altercation and how I felt like this boy was as much at fault as me. Then my dad said, "Sometimes you have to do what you have to do. I do not condone starting a fight, but you do have to defend yourself. If you are in a fight, you better win." And that was the end of the conversation. Whether you agree with that or not, this was the stand my dad took that day. It was very unusual that he did not make a bigger deal of the situation.

Sometime that evening my dad got a phone call from the school explaining that I was in an altercation on the school bus, and I was expelled from riding the bus for a week. We had to find alternate transportation to get me back and forth to school. I had answered the phone, so I knew it was the school when I handed it to my dad. I stood next to him while he had this conversation. When he handed me the phone to return to the hook, he simply said, "It's up to you to find a ride to school. You will not miss any school over this." I was shocked. No punishment, no beating, nothing, well except now it was up to me to find a ride to school. If I missed school because of this, I would really be in trouble. We lived

— TESSICA DAVIS —

about thirty minutes out of town. Nowadays that is no big deal, we drive longer than that for a good burger, but back then it was huge. So, the search was on. I ended up riding to school with a family up the street, the mom and dad were friends with my mom. They were usually running late, and the kids missed the bus a lot anyway, so they agreed to drive me along with their kids to school the following week. Each morning, we had Bible study all the way to school, and in the afternoons, we had Bible study all the way home. Mostly talking about anger and bad choices and so on. For a teenage girl with anger issues, it was a very long week.

It all worked out in the end, but I remember thinking for the first time ever that my dad was cool. He did not lose his temper, yes, I got that honestly. But he did not lose his temper, he did not raise his voice, not at all what I expected him to do. We had a conversation about what, why, and where. I do not remember everything word for word, but it was the first time I can remember actually talking and not arguing with my dad.

Fast forward a few months. In December, the week before Christmas, we lost our house to a fire. So, most of those things that were so important to me (mostly my mom's things) were lost to the flames. We were able to get a few things of my mom's out before our house burned to the ground. It was a total loss. We lost almost everything. Our clothes, our shoes, our books, all gone. Me and my youngest sister were home alone when the fire started, we only managed to get a few things out of the living room before it was too late. We woke up to half of the house already falling in the flames.

Afterward, some of us kids went to live with family members until my dad could get things settled. My brother went and stayed with a friend. I cannot remember exactly

— PATCHWORK OF PURPOSE —

how long that took, but as we were moving into our rented house in the middle of town, my dad got remarried. We moved in along with our new stepmother and her two kids. Still angry and confused about my mother's death, now I had to deal with all these other people that were now supposed to be "family." I tried to stay to myself. It was hard to have conversations because someone would say something that offended the other and the fight was on. I used to tell my friends it was like a war in my house almost every day. At the age of sixteen I left my dad's house in anger. He tried to convince me to return, but my stubbornness would not allow me to. We did not speak again for many years. I was angry, he was angry. It just wasn't a good situation for either one of us. One would think that I had it better staying with an aunt, but the problem was me. It was just as difficult being in her house as it was being in my dad's. But at the time, I would not admit that to anyone, not even myself.

At the age of seventeen, I thought I would be better off on my own and moved out. At this point, I was a senior in high school. I did not see the importance of having my family around me. I did not understand the impact that would make or the toll their absence would take on me. In the months and years to come, I allowed all the family hardships to shape my choices. Some choices were good and some were bad. I had an emptiness in me I did not understand. It caused problems in relationships I would try to maintain. I had forgotten God's teachings. God's word says, "Honor your father and your mother, that your days may be long in the land that the Lord your God is giving you" (Exodus 20:12). My mother always made sure we were at church growing up, but I did not give any weight to it at this time in my life. I wanted to do it on my own. I didn't think I needed anyone. I thought I was better off on my own. No one to answer to, no one telling me what to do; it sounded like a better life. I did not speak to my family for a long time. Not my dad, not my aunt, not my sisters, or my brother. I did not want to hear what they had to say. At the time, their opinions did not matter to me. Little did I know that life has its own challenges.

I know this may have been a hard chapter to read, but I am taking full responsibility for my faults and leaving others with theirs. Some situations cannot be changed, what's done is done. It is in the past, but how you hold on to the negative impacts you. It is your choice to hold on instead of letting go. Sometimes the people around you do not always take the time to understand you or show you love. The good news is that I found a way, with God's guidance, to improve the situation. It is all a matter of choice, as I was saying before. Sometimes we do not want to do the hard work. But as you continue on to the next chapter, you will see it is worth it in the end.

1. **1 Corinthians 13:4-8**—"Love is patient, love is kind. It does not envy, it does not boast, it is not proud. It does not dishonor others, it is not self-seeking, it is not easily angered, it keeps no record of wrongs. Love does not delight in evil but rejoices with the truth. It always protects, always trusts, always hopes, always perseveres. Love never fails. But where there are prophecies, they will cease; where there are tongues, they will be stilled; where there is knowledge, it will pass away"

2. **Proverbs 15:1**—A gentle answer turns away wrath, but a harsh word stirs up anger."

3. **Ephesians 4:26**—"In your anger do not sin: Do not let the sun go down while you are still angry."

4. **Colossians 3:21**—"Fathers, do not embitter your children, or they will become discouraged."

5. **Romans 12:18**—"If it is possible, as far as it depends on you, live at peace with everyone."

As we reflect on the significance of repairing fractured relationships and nurturing bonds of love, we are reminded that the fabric of our lives is intricately woven with the threads of reconciliation. Just as each stitch contributes to the beauty of a quilt, so do our efforts to mend broken bonds and enhance the tapestry of our legacies. In Chapter 6, titled "Threads of Reconciliation: Stitching Together the Legacy of Love," we delve into the profound journey of forgiveness and restoration.

— CHAPTER 6 —
Threads of Reconciliation: Stitching Together the Legacy of Love

After some time had passed, several years in fact, I was married with kids of my own. I found out from one of my sisters that my dad and stepmom had moved to California. He got transferred out there and all their kids were grown and out of the house, so it was a good move for him. He still held on to some land and a home in our hometown and would visit Texas when he could. I would try to call my dad on Father's Day, his Birthday, and the week of Christmas. If he answered, our conversations were mostly short and awkward. He did not know what to say to me and I did not know what to say to him. Over the years, I would hear through the grapevine that he was back in Texas for a visit. He only stopped by my house one time during all his visits. I guess we had grown too far apart and did not know how to get back. Each time I would hear of him being in the state it would hurt me that he wouldn't contact me for a visit. As I think of it now, why would he? We did not have a relationship. I am sure he thought his time was better spent with family and friends he talked to and had a relationship with.

My younger sister stayed in touch with him over the years. She saw a different side to him; or did she? She saw him for who he was. As we get older, we are often able to see our parents as human, capable of mistakes. This is what she was able to see and accept in him. Now do not get me wrong, I am sure they had their own arguments and disagreements. The only difference is, she stayed with him until it was time for her to start her own life and got married herself. She got to know him as an adult. At this point, I did not give him the chance.

After several more years had gone by, all wasted in my opinion, he "retired" and moved back home to Texas. I was feeling convicted to repair what I could of the relationship with my dad. I knew it would have made my mom unhappy to know we did not even speak. I knew it made God unhappy that we had not gotten past all of this. I knew He wanted me to step out and work on this. It had gone on long enough; it was time.

There must be some good in him, after all my mother loved him and, more importantly, God loved him. I decided to start calling and going by his house. Now keep in mind, his house is about an hour's drive to and from where I lived. We (my sisters and I) started planning get-togethers. My oldest sister had moved into a small home on the corner lot of his land, so she was close by. We would gather at her place. A Father's Day cookout. A Birthday BBQ for Dad. Each time we would stay longer and longer, and the conversations would get easier. Sometimes we would get together for no other reason but to be together. Thanksgiving rolled around, and we had this gathering at Dad's house because it was larger. This was the first time I had entered his house in many, many years.

— TESSICA DAVIS —

The last time I saw my dad, it was a hot summer day. We had all gathered there as a family just to spend some time together. Dad got the tractor out and rode down to the pond. He had his rifles and went shooting on the back side of the pond with some of the guys and my sisters. There were snakes in the pond he would use as targets. I do not think they ever shot any. They did not come back celebrating anything, but that is irrelevant. As it was time to make our way back to the house, my sister was driving the tractor and my dad walked back next to me and my husband Danny. It was a good little fifteen-minute walk back. He was pointing out this and that: plans he was making to improve the fence, trees he wanted to clear out and the ones he wanted to make sure and keep. It was the first time I had ever had a conversation like that with him. It was all ease and comfort.

We all made our way back into the house one by one where my stepmom was sitting with her dog. We stayed for a bit longer and decided it was time to get back home. I walked over to my dad, leaned over, told him I loved him, and hugged him. He did not hug me back, (that was just his way) but he did say, "You come back soon, okay?" Wow, what a moment for me. He had never said anything like that to me before. This small little sentence was a huge thing in my life. My dad wanted me in his life. He welcomed me back into his life and invited me to visit him again. What a moment. A few short months later, my dad passed away. I can only take comfort in the fact that the last words we spoke to each other were kind and affectionate.

I would like to ask you to examine your family for a moment. Is there anyone you have not spoken to in a while? Did you have a falling out with someone? Is there someone you have blocked out of your mind? Someone that you thought you were better off without? It may be your mom, your dad, a sister, a brother, a cousin, an aunt, an uncle, it could be someone you were friends with at one time. Is there a broken relationship that can be repaired? It may take a lot of effort on your part, and it may take a long time, but do you think they are worth it? Do you think you are worth it? I know you are thinking, "But they said this," or "They did that." Okay! But we are all human. They may have regrets but do not know how to reopen the lines of communication. Ask God to reveal to you whom He would want you to reconnect with. He will show you the way. He will give you what to say or do.

I can tell you (and will at a different time) that my sisters and I went a long time, many years without speaking. I would tell people that we had nothing to talk about, nothing in common, no common ground, it would be a waste of time, mostly based on opinions I thought they had about me and vice versa. As we began to sit and talk, a little would come out here and there. I know now, that was fear talking. I did not want to face them after everything that was said and done.

We soon realized that they did not think badly of me and I did not feel badly towards them. They were all lies the enemy had planted in our lives. We, my two sisters and I are very close now. We talk a lot more often now than we ever have. We know what is going on in each other's lives and we are there to help each other out when needed. We celebrate our victories and hold the other up during the valleys. I can only imagine what we could have accomplished if we were as close as we are now over all those years. Our low points could have felt like river water, not oceanic waves. Our accomplishments would have been on the highest clouds not just hovering over the treetops. Looking back, the idea that "we have nothing to talk about" has turned into a big joke because we can get on the phone and literally talk all day. We have had conversations that lasted eight to ten hours. It is such a beautiful thing when God restores relationships. The point is: relationships can be repaired. I have seen it. I am living it. It is worth it. They are worth the effort. YOU are worth the effort. God's word says. "Love is patient, love is kind. It does not envy, it does not boast, it is not proud. It does not dishonor others, it is not self-seeking, it is not easily angered, it keeps no record of wrongs. Love does not delight in evil but rejoices with the truth. It always protects, always trusts, always hopes, always perseveres. Love never fails" (1 Corinthians 13:4-8). Relationships are two-sided, but they are worth the work.

Do not think you will make one phone call, send one text or email, and think that everything will be okay. No. It will take work. Some days it will feel like you are doing ALL the work. Do not be defeated. Do not let the lies pile up on you again. Do not allow the enemy to redraw lines. The 'I did this, and they didn't do that' kind of stuff. Do not allow this to take root. Know that what you are fighting for will be worth it in the end. It will take time.

Do you know what they are fighting against? Have you asked them? Are you willing to do your part? It will take effort, REAL EFFORT. Maybe the first encounter is rough and awkward. Well, what did you expect? Of course, it will be. But it's okay. You are opening lines of communication. Be honest with them, not rude, but honest about your feelings. Allow them to be honest with you. Apologize if they feel like you have wronged them, even if you did not know you did. Talk it out. Remember: you are worth it. The enemy wants to keep us apart. If the strong are separated, he thinks he has a chance. When we unite, have open communication, and have concern for each other, we cannot be stopped.

— PATCHWORK OF PURPOSE —

God can use us to break generational influences. He can use us to restore broken souls. He can use us to help those around us. We must put in the time, show effort, and allow God to do His work in and through us. I know that if I had not repaired my relationship with my dad, I would have regretted it for the rest of my life. Even when we were not talking, if someone would bring it up I would just blow it off. Most people thought I did not care at all. But the truth is, it bothered me a lot. It would keep me awake some nights thinking about what I should have done or said. So even if someone comes across as not feeling or not caring, they could be hiding their true feelings. We do not know how long we have on this earth. We are not promised tomorrow. SO, WHAT ARE YOU WAITING ON?

1. **Ephesians 4:31-32**—"Get rid of all bitterness, rage and anger, brawling and slander, along with every form of malice. Be kind and compassionate to one another, forgiving each other, just as in Christ God forgave you."

2. **Colossians 3:13-1**—"Bear with each other and forgive one another if any of you has a grievance against someone. Forgive as the Lord forgave you. And over all these virtues put on love, which binds them all together in perfect unity."

3. **Proverbs 17:9**—"Whoever would foster love covers over an offense, but whoever repeats the matter separates close friends."

4. **Matthew 5:23-24**—"Therefore, if you are offering your gift at the altar and there remember that your brother or sister has something against you, leave

your gift there in front of the altar. First go and be reconciled to them; then come and offer your gift."

As you navigate the complex terrain of family relationships, remember the lessons learned from the story of reconciliation between me and my dad, and also between my sisters and me. Just as a quilt is made up of many different pieces stitched together, our legacies are formed by the relationships we nurture and repair. Let the words of 1 Corinthians 13:4-8 inspire you to take the necessary steps to mend fences, reconcile differences, and leave behind a legacy of love and forgiveness for future generations to inherit.

Remember the choices we make create the patterns we will be remembered for later in life. What is it you want to be remembered for?

"Trust in the Lord with all your heart and lean not on your own understanding; in all your ways submit to Him, and He will make your paths straight."
— *Proverbs 3:5-6*

— CHAPTER 7 —
Divine Encounters: Finding Purpose in Unexpected Moments

One thing that is important to understand is that God can show up anywhere and at any time. He can use people we know, strangers, music, conversations, and many other ways to communicate with us. For example, when I was working at my local car dealership, where I would be in and out of customers' vehicles working in the service department, one of my duties was to get the vehicle information: verify VIN, get mileage, oil life, etc. When getting in the vehicle, I would be subject to whatever the owner had playing on the radio. Not allowed to change their personal settings, sometimes I would just hit the power button and turn the radio off for the duration the vehicle spent in our care. From time to time, I would be in a low spot, having a rough day, or just have lots on my mind. Sometimes it would be the job. Sometimes it would be family drama. Sometimes it would just be that my soul would be searching.

I would enter the vehicle and turn the key just like I had

— PATCHWORK OF PURPOSE —

done hundreds of times before. Then out of nowhere, God starts speaking to me. An old gospel hymn would be playing on the radio or on a CD. A new version of a song I have heard my whole life or a new song I have not been blessed with until now. No matter the day, it was exactly what I needed to hear at that very moment. It would totally change my outlook for the day. After I drove the vehicle around the building, parking it in the appropriate place for its purpose of visiting the facility, I would pause, close my eyes, and enjoy the moment. God was speaking to me again.

I have even been known to say aloud, "Okay, God. I hear you," when the customer is standing there next to me as I gather the needed information. That would most definitely strike up a conversation with them. I sometimes did not even realize I said it out loud. Knowing they just encountered another believer, we would pause our day and share a story or two. As we both walked away to continue the tasks at hand, we were both encouraged. You never know who God is going to put in your path. Sometimes they are there to help you, and sometimes you are meant to help them.

"Be still, and know that I am God;
I will be exalted among the nations,
I will be exalted in the earth."
— Psalm 46:10

As my time continued, I got to know a lot of my customers very well. I believe when you meet someone, you have to offer up a little of yourself to open the gates of communication. Some people appreciated this and some did not. I am not responsible for their thoughts or decisions; I am responsible for doing what I know to be right. From time to time, we would have someone enter our office with a special needs child accompanying them. I have been blessed by having "special" kids in my life. I understand some of their struggles. I would always try to speak to all the kids that entered to help them feel more comfortable about being in a large unfamiliar place. As I saw these families with special children entering, whether they were my customers or one of my co-workers, I would greet the parents and ask the child's name. Most of the time, they would say, "They are not going to talk to you," and I was okay with that. Kneeling, getting on their level, and saying hello using the child's name and telling them my name, I would complement the shirt they were wearing, their shoes, or the toy they were holding in their hand. The child would often hide behind their parent's legs. I would tell them it is okay, and they are not required to speak back to me. I would wish them a good day and then I would turn my attention back to the parents and resume with the purpose of the appointment. Being in a small town, most parents would appreciate this type of greeting.

"Jesus looked at them and said,
'With man this is impossible, but
with God all things are possible.'"
— Matthew 19:26

After they had visited our facility a few times, some of the children would get used to me speaking to them. Sometimes they would just peek around their parent's legs at me with a little smile but one day I got one of the biggest surprises ever. On this particular day, a mom and dad both came in with this beautiful little girl. I treated her like I did all the other children, squatting down to her level to say good morning. The mom told me this little beauty did not

PATCHWORK OF PURPOSE

interact with anyone other than her family. Just as her mom was finishing her sentence, she turned loose of her mom's hand and ran over to me and gave me a huge, arms wrapped around your neck type of hug. It caught me unprepared, and we almost tumbled over. Laughing with pure joy, I was able to recover so we did not hit the floor. The mom stood there with her jaw dropped, I received a blessing this little girl will never know she delivered: the confirmation that I was doing the correct thing. Every child, every person deserves to be spoken to. No one should ever be made to feel like they are not important enough for our time no matter where we are.

Over time, I continued to meet several people who had small children in their lives with one special need or another. They are all different. The child may be their own, a grandchild, a niece/nephew, or even the child of a friend. No matter this child was in their life and their hearts. For some unknown reason to me, these people seem to gravitate toward me. Looking back, I can see it was God. This is scary for a lot of parents. The unknown. What will this child grow up to be? Will they ever overcome enough to function in the world independently? I would simply take a few minutes and share with them the story of my son Brock. I would like to share more of his story with you now.

From Brock's toddler years to preschool, into elementary school, and through his high school years he had many obstacles to overcome. Brock does not have the actual medical diagnosis of Autism but when he was younger, he had a lot of the same challenges. He struggled to overcome several things, but he is a hard worker and we did not give up on him. As a child, he could not follow three-step instructions, his speech was delayed, he would have anger fits, he could not stay focused, he potty trained late, and several other things. Communication was a huge struggle. He would get so frustrated because he could not communicate with us. He has been able to overcome most of these. We found ways around his hurdles of learning by trying new ideas and strategies to help him. Brock learned Philippians 4:13 and would repeat it over and over. "I can do all this through Him who gives me strength" Philippians 4:13. As time progressed, we would have to find alternative ways to teach Brock and communicate with him. It is not that he could not speak or could not hear, it was more of the way he understood things. We had to learn how to explain things in a way that he would understand them.

*"Whether you turn to the right or to the left,
your ears will hear a voice behind you,
saying, 'This is the way; walk in it.'"*
— *Isaiah 30:21*

Brock graduated with his class on time. He did not have to repeat any grades. He attended summer school and before-school tutorials for a few years to help make this happen, but he never complained about the extra time in school. He even passed all the state-required standardized testing that mainstream students are required to pass to graduate. With Brock's IEP (individual education plan) he was not required by the school or the state to even take, much less pass, these tests. As a parent, I could not allow him to take the "easy way out" so I instructed the school to administer the testing just like every other student. As discussed with the administration if he did not receive a passing grade, it would not derail any other plans we had set in place in his IEP. As I said earlier, Brock completed all tests and received passing grades. I did not want to give him an easy out. I

PATCHWORK OF PURPOSE

knew he would one day be a grown man and that this world would not give him anything. We wanted him to learn that sometimes even though it is difficult, you have to work for what you want to accomplish. If you put in the work, it will happen. As a result he walked the stage at graduation with all his friends and classmates. He is holding down a full-time job, independently purchased his first vehicle, and takes care of his finances. He is certified in three different areas of gunsmithing and is now part of the plumber's union. His dream is to own his own business and manufacture his brand of weapons one day. He has a plan and he is working on his plan. I have every confidence he will succeed.

This story alone encouraged so many parents and grandparents. Just to know that it is possible. It is always helpful to talk with someone who has had the same worries or concerns that you have, but they are living on the other side of the answer. God wants us all to be on the other side. He is the answer. He can make it happen. All things are possible according to His Word.

> *"Trust in the Lord with all your heart and lean not on your own understanding; in all your ways submit to Him, and He will make your paths straight."*
> *— Proverbs 3:5-6*

> *"But seek first His kingdom and His righteousness, and all these things will be given to you as well."*
> *— Matthew 6:33*

"WE SERVE A BIG GOD AND HE IS IN CONTROL," is how I would choose to end the story when talking about Brock. Most people would agree. I would always encourage

— TESSICA DAVIS —

them to never stop trying new ideas. With all his other accomplishments, God used my son Brock to teach me a few things as well. Without having Brock in my life, I may not have learned to look at other people the same way God does. This is still difficult for me sometimes, but if we can see others how God sees them, and how Jesus sees them, our entire outlook on them could change. Jesus died for them just as much as He died for me. I am no better than them and they are no better than me when it comes to how Jesus sees us. Sometimes our struggles and victories will encourage others around us. Do not be afraid to share. God has a way of using it all.

Another example: I have been alone in my vehicle driving and my mind starts drifting away. I am no longer paying close enough attention to the road when I hear "Tessica" clear as day as if someone were sitting next to me. As I check my surroundings, I snap back just in time to avoid a collision or make my exit. This has happened to me more times than I can count (I do a lot of driving). My only explanation is God spoke to me. He said my name OUT LOUD to help me. God speaks to us in many ways. Whether it is through His word, a story told by a stranger, a child's embrace, a major victory in your life, or a song on the radio. Open your heart, open your ears, open your eyes, open your understanding; God is all around us. He is there in our good times and in our difficult moments. He is always speaking and always listening. Ask Him to speak to you today.

"Ask and it will be given to you;
seek and you will find; knock and
the door will be opened to you."
— Matthew 7:7

1. **Psalm 46:10**—"Be still, and know that I am God; I will be exalted among the nations, I will be exalted in the earth."

2. **Isaiah 30:21**—"Whether you turn to the right or to the left, your ears will hear a voice behind you, saying, 'This is the way; walk in it.'"

3. **Jeremiah 29:11**—"'For I know the plans I have for you,' declares the Lord, 'plans to prosper you and not to harm you, plans to give you hope and a future.'"

4. **Matthew 19:26**—"Jesus looked at them and said, 'With man this is impossible, but with God all things are possible.'"

As we continue on this journey. It is important to remember that our daily choices help make up the legacy we will leave behind. We choose how we will be remembered. Sharing our struggles and victories with those around us is helpful to them and it also reminds us of God's presence in our lives. As we take the steps into our next chapter, I hope you will examine your life. Is God in your life? Have you asked Jesus to be your Lord and Savior? Do you keep Him at the center of every choice? We all have struggles, but having God on our side makes it easier to navigate.

— CHAPTER 8 —
Patterns of Purpose: Building Your Spiritual Tapestry

I can only imagine you are asking yourself what all the previous chapters have to do with building your life quilt or legacy. If you read chapter one, you know what I am talking about. If you did not, please take time now to do so. This will all become clear very soon.

As we go through our day we create a pattern, a fabric that will be quilted together as our legacy. What choices and decisions are you making to guarantee your quilt will be something beautiful and warm for your family and friends to hold on to?

As you can tell from my pages, I am a believer in Jesus Christ as Lord and Savior. He is molding me and shaping me into who I will ultimately be remembered as. He is using me to help others, to give hope and inspiration in a unique way. It gives me joy and much excitement to see and hear how my struggles and victories have encouraged others. I believe that is why I am here.

— PATCHWORK OF PURPOSE —

If you do not have a personal relationship with my precious Jesus, I encourage you to test His Word. He is the ultimate encourager and healer. If you are wondering how such a relationship can begin, I can help you with that. You cannot walk up to Him in a room at an event you were invited to. I cannot manifest Him so He is standing in front of you. I can tell you from experience how He loves me, how He has changed me, helped me, inspired me, and how He continues to do these things daily.

I can help guide you in your first prayer or conversation to invite Him into your life. He is a gentleman and never imposes on our free will. The choice is yours to make. The first step is for you to believe that Jesus is the Son of God and He came to this earth for you. He died on the cross taking upon Himself all the sin, shame, and hurt of this world. God's word says, "Whoever hears my word and believes Him who sent me has eternal life. He does not come into judgment, but has passed from death to life" (John 5:24).

"For those who find me find life
and receive favor from the Lord."
— Proverbs 8:35

"And the God of all grace, who called you
to His eternal glory in Christ, after you have
suffered a little while, will Himself restore you
and make you strong, firm and steadfast."
— 1 Peter 5:10

"For God so loved the world that He gave His
one and only Son [Jesus], that whoever believes
in Him shall not perish but have eternal life."
— John 3:16

So, if you choose to believe in Jesus and want to make Him Lord and Savior over your life, just read along with me. (If you have already done so, please be patient, continue in this chapter because there is something more we will talk about.)

To welcome Jesus into your life, pray this out loud:

Dear Jesus. I know I was born in sin. I know I am a sinner. I have made poor choices because I have not had you to guide me. I believe you are the son of God and that you died for my sin. I ask you to come into my life, forgive me of my sins, and guide me on the true path that you have laid out for my life. I choose to turn away from sin and follow you. I thank you for your sacrifice at the cross. I thank you for taking my sin from me. I accept you as my Lord and Savior. I thank you for your forgiveness. In Jesus' name, Amen.

Congratulations and welcome to the family. This is a very simple prayer that God will honor; now it is time to join the kingdom. Having Christ in your life does not mean you will never fail or never have any problems in the future. What it does mean is when we do fail, He will be there to help us through. When we fall, He will pick us up. When we need Him, He will be there. I encourage you to find a local church, get involved, and share with them that you have asked Jesus into your heart. They will be able to help you with any questions you may have.

Let us imagine for a second that you invited Christ into your life long ago. It could be a day, week, month, or years ago, but you do not feel His presence. You do not see Him moving in your life. Most people would say He left you. This is not true. He will never leave us. God's word says,

— PATCHWORK OF PURPOSE —

"The Lord Himself goes before you and will be with you; He will never leave you nor forsake you. Do not be afraid, do not be discouraged" (Deuteronomy 31:8).

"So will My word be which goes out of My mouth; It will not return to Me void, Without accomplishing what I desire, And without succeeding in the matter for which I sent it."
— Isaiah 55:11

As we wade through the muddy waters of life, we may make the choice, sometimes unconsciously, to turn away from Him. We think we have a better way. I am a very visual person, so when I start talking about making the change and returning to Him, I imagine myself standing in a room facing the door with Him directly behind me. I can walk through the door, or I can do an about-face, turn one hundred and eighty degrees, and be face-to-face with Him again.

Turn to Him in prayer. Tell Him you realize you are not going along with His plan. Ask for forgiveness for straying away and ask Him for guidance. He is never further away than that. He wants to spend time with you, walk beside you, guide you, and help you along the way. He is waiting for you. He is all-powerful, but He will never force us into a relationship with Him. I can tell you from personal experience, I have had to make the about-face many times. I have had to turn back to God. He was always there waiting for me. His word tells us that He will never leave us. We often think that we have done something or said something that is "too bad" or "too wrong" and that He will not forgive us, but that is a lie from the enemy. Jesus is waiting on us with open arms.

— TESSICA DAVIS —

"My sheep hear my voice, and I know them, and they follow me. I give them eternal life, and they shall never perish; no one will snatch them out of My hand. My Father, who has given them to Me, is greater than all; no one can snatch them out of My Father's hand. I and the Father are one."
— John 10:27-30

When you have something or someone leave your life, it is easy to blame God. The hurt is still present, but He makes it bearable. Think of it like this, God has such great plans for you, but you do not have room for it. How can He give you the things He has without removing others from your life? You cannot have both, it is one or the other. The things we have, we may have worked hard for and it is hard to let go. Think of your life as a filing cabinet. Every piece of paper is valuable. Each one has a purpose and is needed. After a while, the papers are outdated. They do not serve the purpose they were originally intended for. They need to be updated.

This is what God does for us. Our blessings are like these pieces of paper, He removes the old ones to make room for the new ones, the better ones, the ones He has been molding us for. The blessing you are holding on to will not serve you where God is taking you. He is preparing you for something greater.

If you have a smart car, it is great on gas and can be parked in the smallest places. This is great when you are living in a city where space is tight, but if God is moving you out of the city and up to the mountains, this car will not serve its original purpose in your life. You will need an SUV with snow tires to maneuver the roads and terrain God is taking you to.

— PATCHWORK OF PURPOSE —

The smart car was a blessing at the time, but God is planning on giving you something bigger. To do this, the car must go. You no longer need it, so stop holding on to it. You cannot have a smart car in the mountains; He wants to give you a big SUV. Let God purge your life and prepare you for the awesomeness He has in store for you.

Sometimes we have loved ones that are removed from our lives. It could be because of geographics, a lifestyle change, or it can be from death. I have had all three happen to me. I have had friends and family members move away. I have had friendships that just fizzled out because my lifestyle or theirs made a change. It does not matter if the change was on my side or theirs, or if it was a good change or a bad one. All I know is they are no longer part of my life. Maybe later, the season may come when we are needed by each other again. But for now, I must trust the path God has me on and listen when God tells me to make changes.

I have experienced the loss of loved ones due to death. My mom passed away when I was in middle school. I had to find my way without her guidance. I watched my nephew battle cancer and he was taken home to Glory before he was a teenager. I understand loss. We cannot place blame; it is a waste of time and energy that is meant for better things. Sometimes we must accept what is, even when we do not understand why it happened.

No matter the reason, that person was important to us during that season of our life. The lessons we learned from them will always be with us. The laughs and the tears we shared with them will mold us into who we are becoming. They were here to help us, they completed their task, and now God has a different plan for them and you.

No matter if you are new to the kingdom, if you are faithful in your relationship, or even if you have turned away from God, He is always there for you. He will never leave us. He is waiting for us. He has many things He is trying to give us, but we must allow it. Remember that the choices we make create patterns. Today's pattern could be bright and vibrant, and tomorrow's could be thin and lack color. Each day, and with each choice, we decide how we will be remembered

On our best days, we helped someone who needed it, we gave a compliment, or we encouraged. Maybe we stopped in the middle of our busy day and prayed with a stranger. Maybe we made sure God was in our every thought and decision. These are days where we have created patterns that will bring someone joy. These are patterns that will give our loved ones warmth when we are no longer here with them.

It is the days that we do not make the best choices we have to watch out for. We all make mistakes. We all do things unintentionally. We all have days where we do not put our best selves out there. Some days we can just be complacent, and not do anything to hurt anyone, but being complacent is not where God wants us to be.

Our pattern for the day will not bring joy to those we leave behind. The pattern/fabric will be there as part of our quilt, but we must make sure we have more bright, vibrant, thick patterns so the focus and memories will be pleasant and uplifting to God. What is your pattern looking like today? We cannot go back and change the yesterdays, but we have all the power to make sure our tomorrows and todays are what we want them to be, what we want to be remembered as.

You are not alone. God is with you. He will put the correct people in your path and in your life to help you on this journey. Trust in Him. "Trust in the Lord with all thine heart; and lean not on your own understanding. In all your

— PATCHWORK OF PURPOSE —

ways acknowledge Him, and He shall direct your paths." (Proverbs 3:5-6)

1. **Ephesians 2:10** — "For we are God's handiwork, created in Christ Jesus to do good works, which God prepared in advance for us to do."

2. **Romans 8:28** — "And we know that in all things God works for the good of those who love Him, who have been called according to His purpose."

3. **Psalm 139:13-14** — "For You created my inmost being; You knit me together in my mother's womb. I praise You because I am fearfully and wonderfully made; Your works are wonderful, I know that full well."

4. **Jeremiah 29:11** — "'For I know the plans I have for you,' declares the Lord, 'plans to prosper you and not to harm you, plans to give you hope and a future.'"

5. **Proverbs 16:9** — "In their hearts humans plan their course, but the Lord establishes their steps."

As we bring this chapter to an end, we have woven together the threads of our choices and beliefs, forming the fabric of our legacy. As we reflect on the patterns we create each day, it's clear that our actions and decisions contribute to the quilt of our lives. Whether consciously or unconsciously, we are crafting a narrative that will be remembered by those we leave behind.

Now, let's delve deeper into Chapter 9, "Comfortable Conversations: Building Uplifting Relationships." Just as we seek comfort in the spaces we inhabit, we also crave comfort in our interactions with others. Yet, like sitting on uncom-

— TESSICA DAVIS —

fortable furniture, conversations and relationships can leave us feeling uneasy if not approached with care and intentionality. Let's explore how we can create spaces of warmth and welcome in our interactions, nurturing relationships that uplift and inspire.

"Therefore, if anyone is in Christ, he is a new creation. The old has passed away; behold, the new has come."
— 2 Corinthians 5:17

— CHAPTER 9 —
Comfortable Conversations: Building Uplifting Relationships

Have you ever been to a friend or loved one's home and sat on their furniture just to find out that it is very uncomfortable? You may give it some time and move seats. *This chair hurts my back, that chair is too hard, I am afraid this one will break if I sit in it.* To the eyes, it is all appealing and very nice to look at. The colors are vibrant, and the room is arranged well, but you just cannot get comfortable. Conversations and relationships can be the same.

If you are talking with someone and their language is foul, it is hard to listen to the content. They may have some very important information, something that could change your life, but you cannot get comfortable in the conversation.

> *"Let no corrupting talk come out of your mouths, but only such as is good for building up, as fits the occasion, that it may give grace to those who hear."*
> *— Ephesians 4:29*

— PATCHWORK OF PURPOSE —

I have a niece. She is in her early twenties and she is very beautiful. She has long black hair, naturally tan skin, big beautiful brown eyes, and straight teeth that shine when she smiles. Her laugh is infectious. She is tall and thin and can wear any style of clothes she wants, and she will look amazing in it. To look at her, you would think she is the type of person you would want to talk to. She is very approachable. Now keep in mind, I said she is my niece and I love her unconditionally, However, when she opens her mouth to speak, I cringe. One of her favorite adjectives is the "F" bomb and she uses it in almost every breath. The subject matter does not matter. For some people, this would not matter but for me, I cannot get past it. At one point in my life, I have to admit, it was in fact the most used word in my vocabulary, but now God has changed me. He has changed how I speak and I do not want to hear all the flab talk. The sentence fillers if you will. I cannot get comfortable in those conversations. I choose, because I love her, to sit and talk with her anyway. However, I do not feel like I gain anything from it. It is quite the opposite. It is very draining for me to listen to the "F" bombs and all the negativity that goes with it.

> *"But now you must put them all away: anger, wrath, malice, slander, and obscene talk from your mouth."*
> *— Colossians 3:8*

Recognizing this has made me stop and think. When I speak, how does it make others feel? Are the conversations, language, and topics welcoming or off-putting? Am I uplifting the person or dragging them down? Is the other person energized or drained? Are they, am I, improved at the end of the conversation? Stop and think about that for a minute.

Do your conversations have people wanting to come back and talk with you again or is it more of a chore for them? Do they get joy when they see your name and phone number come across the caller ID or do they roll their eyes and think to themselves, "What is it now?" Are you surrounded by people who speak that way, so it helps you feel comfortable in it? Have you ever thought about it? I have to admit, that before I was writing this, I had not given it much thought. We all have areas we need to improve. Is this one of those areas for you?

> *"A soft answer turns away wrath,*
> *but a harsh word stirs up anger."*
> — *Proverbs 15:1*

Friendships or relationships can fall under the same pattern. I had a "friend" at one time that was exhausting. The relationship was exhausting. She had a way of making me feel important at the beginning of the friendship. That is what we all want from our friends, isn't it? Isn't that why we befriend them in the first place? They make us feel valuable. She had some drama in her life like we all do in some form or fashion. So, I would try to help her with it. Having someone on your side is always helpful. However, as time went on, her drama seemed to increase and be the most important thing. It seemed to be all we talked about. When I would bring up an issue I was having and needed some advice, she did not seem very interested. She would listen, but soon the conversation would turn back to her drama and how her circumstances were much worse or more important at the time. So, I ask you this: at what point do you back away from a relationship? At what point do you see that this is not the person God intended you to be spending time with?

— PATCHWORK OF PURPOSE —

Sometimes we allow others in our life that God did not intend on being there. They will not help us get to where we are going. They do not see the plans we have. They cannot dream the dreams God intended for us.

> *"One who is righteous is a guide to his neighbor,*
> *but the way of the wicked leads them astray."*
> *— Proverbs 12:26*

My "friend" was having legal issues with some of her family members. They were stalking her house and some of her friends, including me, trying to keep tabs on her. I was at her home one day and the cops arrived. They basically said to me that if I did not want to be involved, I needed to leave that instant. This was not their first visit, and they knew all the previous circumstances enough to know I was not part of it. I did not want to get involved with the cops and this legal battle and whatever else she had going on, so I left as they instructed. At that point, I felt like I was getting dragged in by the neck. So, I had to cut the rope. I would still talk to her on the phone from time to time but never went back to her house. When we did talk, I would limit the conversation to work, kids, vacations, and things like that. I would no longer talk about or be involved with her drama.

> *"Do not be deceived: 'Bad*
> *company ruins good morals.'"*
> *— 1 Corinthians 15:33*

I found out quickly that she could not have a conversation that did not involve the drama and she would soon stop calling. After the calls stopped, I realized I had a weight lifted off me. I did not realize her drama was weighing me down. This was a toxic relationship. My "friend" was not a friend at all. She fueled herself on the drama. She would portray herself as the victim but would continuously stir the pot that would fuel the fire. This way the others would retaliate, and she would appear to be the victim. If she did not have drama, she would create some. This way those around her, her friends, would feel sorry for her. She would feed on the negative drama to get others to tell her how great she was for dealing with it all "with class." What they did not see was she was creating it. She would only let them see a portion of the situation. I got close enough for God to show me the truth.

> *"Make no friendship with a man given to anger, nor go with a wrathful man, lest you learn his ways and entangle yourself in a snare."*
> — *Proverbs 22:24-25*

God showed me she was not a friend at all. She was looking for another enabler and sympathetic ear. I found myself no longer comfortable in the friendship. It was like sitting in a chair that was full of rocks. Each time I was there, I seemed to get a pinch or a stick. Everything was off kilter. It was painful to be there. After spending more time with God than with her, He created an exit. I pray that God does a work in her and she is healed in the name of Jesus.

Now, let me ask you this. Have you ever had someone come over, kick their shoes off, and just snuggle up on the sofa, or walk into the kitchen and open the fridge to see what they can fine? I have. They walk in and just make themselves at home. It is a great feeling to know that the space that I call home could be comfortable enough for people to do this. Is it the space or is it the environment? Is it that my sofa is just that comfortable (I can assure you it is not) or is it more

— PATCHWORK OF PURPOSE —

likely this person is so comfortable with me, that they know they will not be judged for just being themselves? That is the kind of person I want to be. That is the kind of environment I want to create wherever I go. This comfy sofa wraps around people to help them feel welcome and warm like they have a home. I want to be the person who wraps people with the love of Jesus, helps them relax, and allows them to (open that fridge and) reach for their goals. It is important to not allow others to dump their rocks on you, the negativity they have surrounding them and the bitterness they hold on to. You cannot let that affect you. I want the environment around me to remain soft and comfy for those relationships where we grow together. Both parties must be comfortable in the relationship for it to be successful. I want to help those around me succeed. I want to see them grow. I want to help cheer them on.

I do not wish anyone any harm. If they have been inside my circle of friends and influence and are no longer in that position for whatever reason, I only wish for the best in their lives. Maybe the circumstances will change and we will be close again, but until then: I pray for those who have not found the peace of God. I pray they will lean into Him and His Word and find their purpose. I pray they will allow God to do a mighty work in their life. And I pray they will use their testimony to share the love of Jesus.

> *"If possible, so far as it depends on you, live peaceably with all."*
> *— Romans 12:18*

No matter if it is a conversation, relationship, or a passing glance, I want others to see the love of Christ in me. I want my daily fabrics to show how much God has given me and how well I embrace my purpose for Him. What about you? What do you want your daily life and/or conversations to look and feel like? Are you the kind of person people can easily talk with or feel comfortable around? This was not always the case for me. I had to work on myself and allow God to work on me. I no longer wanted my conversations and relationships to be filled with rocks. I wanted to be comfortable (not complacent) in my relationships.

> *"Finally, all of you, have unity of mind, sympathy, brotherly love, a tender heart, and a humble mind."*
> — 1 Peter 3:8

What do you need or want to change in your life? Don't feel like just because you make changes, others will always see the negative in you. That is where I stayed for a long time. I felt like it wouldn't matter one way or another. Then God showed me that it did matter. It mattered to Him. It mattered to me. Over time, others will see the changes in you. Don't let fear of what others think hold you back. Are others seeing you like God sees you? Do you have enough Jesus in your life that others can see? All you have to do is keep your eyes on Christ, make one small change at a time as He leads you to, and let God work on the rest. Over time, you can and will become the person you want to be, and the person God intended you to be, a person full of love and compassion.

> *"Therefore, if anyone is in Christ, he is a new creation. The old has passed away; behold, the new has come."*
> — 2 Corinthians 5:17

— PATCHWORK OF PURPOSE —

1. **Philippians 4:8**—"Finally, brothers and sisters, whatever is true, whatever is noble, whatever is right, whatever is pure, whatever is lovely, whatever is admirable—if anything is excellent or praiseworthy—think about such things."

2. **Galatians 6:2**—"Carry each other's burdens, and in this way you will fulfill the law of Christ."

3. **James 1:19**—"My dear brothers and sisters, take note of this: Everyone should be quick to listen, slow to speak and slow to become angry."

4. **Proverbs 27:17**—"As iron sharpens iron, so one person sharpens another."

5. **Matthew 5:16**—"In the same way, let your light shine before others, that they may see your good deeds and glorify your Father in heaven."

Continuing the exploration of divine communication and intimacy, focusing on a relationship with God, Chapter 10 invites you to reflect on the ways in which God speaks to individuals in moments of quiet intimacy rather than grand theatrical displays. Contrasting the allure of sensational stories of divine intervention and the gentle whispers of God's presence through personal anecdotes and biblical reflections, Chapter 10 encourages you to embrace the stillness and listen for the whispers of God's guidance and presence in your lives, echoing Psalms 46:10's call to "Be still, and know that I am God." Join me as we continue into the next chapter.

CHAPTER 10
The Whisper of God: Finding Intimacy in His Presence

Have you had the pleasure of talking to someone or listening to a speaker who has had a miraculous moment with God? They tell the story with such passion and joy. It is very intense. You sit on the edge of your seat as you picture the story in your head. Watching it unfold like a movie. It has a good plot, a great lead character, and twists and turns. Then the scene comes where they take your breath away with the big reveal as they describe the moment in which God swoops in and changes everything. He takes the pain, the addictions, and the sadness and replaces it all with this indescribable joy and heavenly happiness. You know what I mean.

I have seen many stories told. I have been to many events where someone is standing on stage getting a word from God, picking someone out of the crowd and giving them a revelation from God, a breakthrough, confirmation, prayers for healing, or specific encouragement. Often sitting in these environments, I am struggling with my own issues. Fear, faith, finances (or lack thereof), low self-esteem, feeling inadequate, the list goes on and on. I remember feeling like God has forgotten me. I remember asking, "God, when is it my turn? Don't you see me? Am I not important enough to experience the same thing?" Secretly I was jealous of these other people, knowing God stepped in, showed up, and spoke to them in a BIG way, A public way. I have secretly struggled with this for years. I would never share this with anyone. What I did not understand at the time was God was speaking to me, but I could not hear Him because I would not shut up and get out of my own mind. What God had for me was much sweeter.

God does not always speak in a loud roar. He does not always use thunder, lightning, smoke, lights, or rolling clouds. Sometimes, oftentimes, He speaks in a whisper. The big theatricals are great, an awesome way to capture a person's attention. They are a way to shock people out of a distracting or destructive path. They are fascinating testimonials. They are the wow factor that most of us look for, however, by looking and waiting on the theatrical, we often miss the whispers.

Do you remember as a child, when your parent or loved one whispered something in your ear? Just the act of them taking the time to do so would make you smile. Most of the time it did not even matter what was said. The act, the closeness, feeling their breath against your skin would bring joy to you. The feeling that you had a secret just the two of you. God wants to speak to us in that same way.

As a child, my son Brock would have physical outbursts. He would kick and scream, hit his head on the walls and floor. This was due to a medical condition and there was no medication (that I was willing to let him put in his body) that would help. So, I had to find a way to calm him without hurting him or him hurting me. I would put him in my lap facing away from me, tuck his legs between mine, wrap my arms around him holding his arms and hands down as I whispered in his ear. I would tell him how loved he is, how proud of him I am, how much I understand his frustration, and sometimes I would sing. During this process to an outsider, it would look like I was torturing him. In reality, I was preventing him from hurting himself, hurting me, and hurting others. After a while, he would start to settle. The screams would not be as loud, the struggling and trying to get away would ease up. I would not let go yet; if I let go too early, it would all start over again. Even though I was totally exhausted, I still held on and whispered, sang, whatever seemed to be working at the moment. Until it came. The big sigh, the deep breath, and the total relaxation of his arms and legs. Once he was totally relaxed, quiet, and calm I released my grip. I loosened my arms, but I never stopped whispering to him. He would just sit in my lap with his head resting on my chest listening to me until he was satisfied that everything was going to be okay. Sometimes this would be five minutes and sometimes it would be thirty minutes. It would depend on him.

    I tell you the story about my son because I have discovered that God works the same way. Had I approached my son with a big roar or a large theatrical performance, the problem would not have been solved. In fact, it would have only gotten worse. He would not have understood what was going on. He would have fought against it. He would not have felt the security of my arms or heard my voice. If we are screaming, we cannot hear. If we are doing all the talking, we cannot hear. Even if it were theatrical, we could not hear over our own voice, we could not see past our

– PATCHWORK OF PURPOSE –

own creation of flags waving and lights flashing. We do not have to do these things to get God's attention. Don't get me wrong, I am not talking about large gatherings, church services, revivals, or things of that nature. At my home church, we have some awesome praise and worship sessions. Some are loud, bright, and big (and I love it), but some are more low-key, quiet, and intimate. I am not talking about corporate worship where we are all together, I am talking about our time with God. The time we spend with Him alone.

I have learned that God speaks to me in whispers. He comes to me in a more intimate way. He wraps His arms around me, allowing me to feel His presence and hear His voice. When we are in the middle of a light show, the intimacy can be lost. Instead of screaming, waving my flags, and looking for the theatrical, I should just relax, take a deep breath, and realize that God is whispering to me. He wants me to understand that things are going to be okay. He wants intimate time with me. I like to sit in a quiet room, open my ears, and open my heart. I may not get a revelation each time, but I do walk away with a full heart and with a clear mind. Sometimes I must admit, I have my praise and worship music on loud and I am singing and dancing around the kitchen, and I believe God honors that as well. You see it is all about the heart. My heart is open, my ears are open, and I am praising my Savior. I feel His presence all over me and that is how I know it is just Him and me in that moment. It is the same feeling I have at church when we are raising our hands and worshiping together. If I were doing it as a show, to impress someone else, that would be different; I do not believe God would honor that. I do it for God. It is my time with Him and it does not matter to me if I am by myself or in a room full of people. Some of you may not believe in the dancing and the hand raising, and that is okay. It is just how I choose to worship my King.

What is it you are wanting from God? Is it the big theatrical event, where He swoops down and fixes everything in a single moment? Is it the intimacy of being in His presence and hearing the softness of His voice? Is it the gentleness of His forgiveness? There is no right or wrong in what we want, however, it is the relationship with Him that He wants. What is more important to you, what you want or what He wants? God's word says, "Come to Me, all you that labor and are heavy burdened, and I will give you rest. Take My yoke (or harness) upon you and learn from Me, for I am gentle and humble in heart, and you will find rest for your souls" (Matthew 11: 28-29).

Additionally, Psalms 46:10 states, "Be still, and know that I am God; I will be exalted among the nations, I will be exalted in the earth." This verse emphasizes the importance of quieting ourselves before God to hear His whispers and experience His presence.

1. **1 Kings 19:11-12**—"The Lord said, 'Go out and stand on the mountain in the presence of the Lord, for the Lord is about to pass by.' Then a great and powerful wind tore the mountains apart and shattered the rocks before the Lord, but the Lord was not in the wind. After the wind, there was an earthquake, but the Lord was not in the earthquake. After the earthquake came a fire, but the Lord was not in the fire. And after the fire came a gentle whisper."

2. **Isaiah 30:21**—"Whether you turn to the right or to the left, your ears will hear a voice behind you, saying, 'This is the way; walk in it.'"

3. **Psalm 37:7**—"Be still before the Lord and wait patiently for Him; do not fret when people succeed in their ways, when they carry out their wicked schemes."

4. **James 4:8**—"Draw near to God, and He will draw near to you."

5. **John 10:27**—"My sheep listen to My voice; I know them, and they follow Me."

Having a personal relationship with God, being able to hear His voice, and spending intimate time with Him prepares us for the plans He has for us. As we continue our exploration, we shift our focus to the profound impact that one individual can make, even in the face of adversity. This next chapter will show you how living your life every day in the presence of God will open opportunities to share the love of God. Chapter 11 introduces you to Brennan Daigle, whose story serves as a testament to the extraordinary ways in which God can work through ordinary people. God has made us all special, even if we view ourselves as "ordinary." He did not call us to be ordinary, He made us to be extraordinary. He created us to stand apart and be different from this world. Join us as we witness the transformative power of faith and love in Brennan's life and discover how his legacy continues to inspire others to live out their faith boldly.

CHAPTER 11
Brennan's Legacy: A Journey of Impact and Inspiration

If you are anything like me, you have had thoughts of how "small" our life is compared to this big world we live in. Thoughts of impacting the world can be scary and near impossible to fathom. God has created us to have large lives in our own way. He has created us all unique, with our own gifts and abilities. As we deal with our ups and downs, how can we make an impact so big that the only explanation must be that God himself ordained it? The only explanation is God ordered the steps giving us our highs and allowing our (what we see as) lows. The story I want to share with you is very personal to me and my family. There are not enough words on this planet to fully explain the impact one person made. My nephew Brennan Wade Daigle made an impact so big that his story and his testimony are shared nationwide. This story is my account of his situation based on my memories and timelines.

My story of Brennan will begin when he was in fourth

grade and eight years old. His mom, dad, and school started to notice a change in him. Where he was once the little boy who would jump out of bed happy and ready to go to school, he was no longer interested in school. He simply did not want to go. He didn't want to go see his friends. He started acting out when his mom and dad would drop him off at school. He started having major disciplinary concerns. He also started complaining of headaches.

After several doctor appointments, the news was delivered that Brennan had a tumor at the base of his brain. He was diagnosed with a rare form of cancer. His team of doctors at Texas Children's Hospital quickly came up with a plan for treatment and started scheduling visits. As surgery was not an option, his schedule for treatments was very intense. His treatments are not the point of this story. That is for another time. I would like to share with you my account, my memories of this little boy, and how he changed my thinking. I do not recall how it all came about; I do not recall all the dates and times when things happened. What I do remember is the impact this one little boy made. I am telling you this story from my perspective, the way I remember the events. Brennan's story can be found in several places on the web. After you read my memories of him, I encourage you to search for him on the web and see for yourself.

My sister and I had many conversations over the phone talking about how the community she lived in was "coming together" to help them, befriend them, and show support. I always thought that it was a cool thing but I often thought she had embellished the stories a little. I remember thinking that if it made her feel better, if it helped her deal with this impossible situation, then a little embellishment was okay. This was before cell phones were in every hand and social media was a way of communication. Our calls were long-distance and the charges would soon begin to add up. She lived about an hour away, so I did not see firsthand what she was explaining. I did not understand the impact God was creating before our very eyes. I was told stories about how Brennan was playing video games "online" with different people. Not understanding how it all worked (because this was before it was happening in almost every home in America), I just dismissed its significance. Later I found out Brennan and his mom and dad were playing games online with soldiers. Men in the military were taking the time to play online with this little guy. I began to think, this is weird. Why would they do that? The answer shocked me. Brennan was talking with them about himself, his situation, and more importantly his God. It was not all about the games, it was more about the connections. Brennan, his mom, and his dad had made these connections and built relationships with these men and women who were serving our country.

We made the drive across the state line from Texas to Louisiana to join them for a community event. Afterward, we decided to all go out together for dinner. After arriving at the restaurant, we all (about fifteen of us) were getting the kids settled at the table, figuring out where everyone would sit. As I looked around, I noticed Brennan and Kristy (his mom, my sister) were missing. I asked if anyone knew where they were. I was shocked when I got a reply. I do not even remember who answered, but Kristy and Brennan stayed outside because he was getting a phone call. Such a simple thing, but who was on the other end of the call? A soldier deployed in Afghanistan. He was one of their new friends who played online with Brennan and who would sit and talk about how great our God is with Brennan. He took the time to give Brennan a call and check in on him.

— PATCHWORK OF PURPOSE —

My sister had gotten a cell phone for this very reason. She wanted a way for people to be able to get in touch with her or Brennan at any time. Especially the doctors.

As I was asking about these phone calls later, I found out that several soldiers would call and check in. They all would give inspiration to each other in different ways. You see, even though Brennan was dealing with chemo, radiation, pain, and everything that goes along with it, Brennan would always find a way to let the people around him know how much God loves them and how much Jesus meant to him. The call that particular day lasted a good twenty to thirty minutes. I remember thinking how awesome it was that this soldier from so far away would take some of his free time to spend on the phone with a nine-year-old little boy.

Brennan's story began to spread. Not only about his treatments but how he, as this little boy, was bringing people together and sharing the love of Jesus. I was sitting at work one day, where the news would play all day in the background. I turned around to look at the TV because I heard the name Brennan Daigle. The way the room was designed when sitting at my desk, my back would be to the TV. As I did not listen to the news very often, this worked in my favor. On this day, it was different. I completely stopped working and started telling everyone to stop working and look at the TV. My boss came out of his office, annoyed, asking what was going on. I was standing in the middle of the room telling him to turn up the TV. They were talking about my nephew on national television. A very popular and political influencer was talking about my nephew and the impact he was making in this world.

As Brennan's tenth birthday was approaching, he told his mom he wanted to have a G.I. Joe-themed birthday party. As his diagnosis was terminal, the family wanted to make this the "party of all parties." Everyone already knew Brennan wanted to join the Army after graduating high school so having a G.I. Joe party was understandable. With help from some new friends, the phone calls started. The venue was arranged, and a call was made to the nearby Army base and an invitation was extended to any soldiers who would like to attend. Thinking a handful of family-oriented men and women would show, it turned into something on a much grander scale. The military commanding officer at the base had to limit the number of soldiers that could come because there was an overabundance of men and women who volunteered to attend. His story was known at the base and the response was overwhelming. We had forty soldiers show up to the birthday party of this ten-year-old boy. The venue was full of family and friends, but as the soldiers began to arrive, it was simply breathtaking. It was a convoy of military vehicles of all sizes filled with soldiers. As an act of kindness, they had a private ceremony where they swore Brennan into the United States Army with the rank of colonel. This allowed him to out-rank some of the soldiers that were present. Brennan was weak from his illness, but they were very gracious and with a smile on their face would "drop and do twenty" pushups as ordered by Brennan in his small and frail voice. They all brought him gifts that consisted of metals they had earned, blankets, water bottles, cards, cash, fatigues, and backpacks full of different things. They lined up and waited patiently until each of them had a few minutes with Brennan giving him his gifts, sharing happy wishes, and saluting him as a fellow soldier and an officer before walking away. This was the most amazing thing I have ever seen. These grown men and women, fighting to keep us all free, wanted to give up their free time to come and meet this young boy because they were inspired.

— PATCHWORK OF PURPOSE —

I have many stories I can tell about this young man and the impact he made, but I will try to keep it to a minimum. One of my favorite stories is one told by his mom. One day as they were talking about the love of Jesus, Kristy asked Brennan what he thought heaven would be like. One of his responses was that it must have duct tape and overalls, a simple answer from a country boy. Now I am sure Kristy tells the story with a lot more detail and probably with more clarity and emotion. I just mention it because it shows a little of his personality. In his mind duct tape could fix anything.

I have a photo, one of my most treasured, where Brennan was lying on the sofa and Kristy was sitting on the floor, back to the sofa with her arm extended out holding his hand with Brennans' favorite stuffed animal laying on her shoulder. After months and months of treatments, ups and downs, they were preparing for Brennan to go home and be with his best friend, Jesus. Kristy would not leave his side.

As they called in hospice, they turned the living room into a temporary hospital room to help with the care of Brennan. Kristy would not leave his side (not even to eat, not to sleep) for days. She would sleep in the chair next to him if she wasn't in the bed with him. She tells the story of laying in the bed with him as he labored to breathe. Kristy lay there telling him that it was okay to go. It was okay to go with Jesus, reassuring him that she and the rest of the family would be okay. God would take care of us all. She whispered it to him over and over until he took his last breath here on earth.

The days that followed consisted of the largest funeral I have ever seen. This huge church was packed, with miles of cars, trucks, motorcycles, etc. taking him to his final resting place. Friends and family gathered to give their sympathies. There is not much more I can say on this other than it has been the single most difficult thing I have had to watch. My sister had to let go of her son on this side of heaven. We still talk about him, laugh at his silliness, and are overwhelmed by the wisdom this young man had. He had such an understanding of the love of Jesus. I can only hope I can reach that same level one day.

Now with all this being said, please tell me how we have the right to say we live small lives, that our life does not matter? This ten-year-old boy shared the love of Jesus with everyone he spoke to and he was able to reach people overseas and was talked about on national television. Why do we think our reach is any shorter? You may be thinking that he had a better story. Well, I am here to tell you that he had a different story, not better. God will use what we have. Our gifts, our abilities, our weaknesses, our stories, they all come from God. Why does across town feel so impossible? No matter your circumstances, no matter your story, someone is waiting to hear from you. Someone is watching to see God in you. Big. Small. Those are just words. God has ordained our steps. Our stories will all be different, but all as important as the ones told before and after.

Don't you think I had some of those same reservations when I started this project? As I mentioned in an earlier chapter, the enemy was giving me every reason he could think of so I would not proceed. Even now as I am writing, going through the editing phases, and preparing to launch he is trying to get to me. All we can do is trust in God. Trust that His ways are higher, His thoughts are higher, His plan is better, and His faithfulness is greater than anything we or the enemy can conjure up. We have no excuses; all He asks from us is to take that step in faith. We don't need to know all the plans; all we need to know is the next step. Whatever it is that God is telling you, take that step.

— PATCHWORK OF PURPOSE —

God's word says, "Go therefore and make disciples of all nations, baptizing them in the name of the Father and of the Son and of the Holy Spirit, and teaching them to obey everything that I have commanded you. And remember, I am with you always, to the end of the age" (Matthew 28: 19-20).

"But you should control yourself at all times, accept troubles, do the work of telling the Good News, and complete all the duties of a servant of God" (2 Timothy 4:5). "Preach the Good News. Be ready at all times..." (2 Timothy 4:2).

The only person that can fulfill the purpose God assigned you is YOU! Step into your destiny. Step into your legacy.

1. **Philippians 4:13**—"I can do all things through Him who strengthens me."—This scripture emphasizes the strength and empowerment we receive from God to fulfill our purpose and make an impact, even in the face of challenges. This was Brennan's favorite scripture.

2. **1 Peter 4:10**—"Each of you should use whatever gift you have received to serve others, as faithful stewards of God's grace in its various forms."—This scripture highlights the importance of using our unique gifts and abilities to serve others and make a positive impact in the world, just as Brennan did.

3. **Matthew 5:16**—"In the same way, let your light shine before others, that they may see your good deeds and glorify your Father in heaven."—This scripture encourages us to let our actions reflect God's love and goodness, ultimately bringing glory to Him, similar to how Brennan's life reflected the love of Jesus.

4. **Romans 8:28**—"And we know that in all things God works for the good of those who love Him, who have been called according to His purpose."—This scripture reassures us that even in the midst of trials and tribulations, God is working for our good and fulfilling His purpose in our lives, as He did in Brennan's life.

5. **Jeremiah 29:11**—"'For I know the plans I have for you,' declares the Lord, 'plans to prosper you and not to harm you, plans to give you hope and a future.'" — This scripture reminds us of God's sovereign plan for our lives, filled with hope and purpose, even when we may face difficulties.

After recounting the remarkable impact of Brennan Daigle's life in Chapter 11, we now turn our attention to the broader theme of living testimonies in Chapter 12. Just as Brennan's story served as a powerful example of God's love in action, we explore how each of us can become living testimonies, spreading God's love and grace through our own lives.

"But in your hearts honor Christ the Lord as holy, always being prepared to make a defense to anyone who asks you for a reason for the hope that is in you; yet do it with gentleness and respect." — 1 Peter 3:15

— CHAPTER 12 —
Living Testimonies: Sharing God's Love through Our Lives

In the unshakable foundation of our lives lies our unwavering belief in God Almighty. For my husband and me, this belief is paramount. We immerse ourselves in the Word of God, embracing His truths and steadfastly holding onto our faith. Now is the time for us to spread the love of God to those around us. It's time to share our testimonies, victories, and lives.

When we speak of testimony as Christians, it's often associated with the moment we invited Christ into our lives, the beginning of our journey with Him. But let's reconsider the term "testimony." It's not confined to a single moment; it's an ongoing narrative. Just as the scriptures unfold, so does our testimony. It grows with every step we take, every decision we make, and every challenge we overcome. Our testimony is a dynamic reflection of our lives, evolving as we grow in faith.

Consider this: can a solitary moment of kneeling in

prayer truly motivate others? While such moments hold personal significance, our testimonies encompass far more. They're not just about conversion but about transformation, encompassing our failures, mistakes, and victories. Instead of dwelling on a singular experience, we should share how God continually shapes, forgives, heals, and guides us. It's through our ongoing journey that we inspire others to walk in faith. It is a victorious moment when a person gives their life to the Lord. As they ask Him to shape them and guide them, it is that moment when the angels shout praises in heaven. I ask you this, how much greater is it when it can be told about how Jesus freed someone from an addiction? How much greater is it when someone can say that He comforted them when they were grieving? How much hope does it spread when we tell of all the great and mighty things God has done for us? Yes, salvation is a beautiful thing and if that is all I received from God, it is still more than I deserve. But our God not only wants salvation for us, He wants a relationship. He wants to bless us. He wants to help us and guide us. He wants us to go share all the good things He has done for us and through us.

> *"But be doers of the Word, and not hearers only, deceiving yourselves."*
> — James 1:22

This emphasizes the importance of living out our faith and sharing our ongoing testimonies, not merely recounting past experiences.

God has bestowed upon us a voice to proclaim His love, not to remain silent. Let us not succumb to defeat but rather share our stories, extending love to others through our words and actions. In times of despair and uncertainty, our testimonies serve as beacons of hope. Each of us is placed precisely where God intends, entrusted with unique experiences to touch hearts and uplift souls. It's not merely our neighbor's or friend's testimony that can inspire; it's ours—the voice of our own journey—that carries the most profound impact. You may be thinking that you are just a regular person and you don't have any of the big stories to tell. But you do. Did you eat today? Did you sleep in a warm bed? Did you have clothes to wear? Did you have clean water to drink? Do you have family and friends around you?

He saved you. He has provided for you. He has comforted you. He has healed your sickness. He has made Himself available to you. These are the things we can share with each other. Give Him praise in and for everything.

"In the same way, let your light shine before others, so that they may see your good works and give glory to your Father who is in heaven."
— Matthew 5:16

This verse encourages us to share our testimonies through our actions, letting our lives reflect the glory of God. Jesus declared in Matthew 10:33, "Whoever denies Me before men, I also will deny before My Father who is in heaven." Let us heed His words and boldly proclaim His Truth. Let us be vocal, unafraid to share our lives, our testimonies, and the good news of His grace and mercy. May our voices resound with His love, echoing through the hearts of all who listen.

I would like to share with you the testimony of how this book came about. God woke me up early one morning and encouraged me to leave the house so I could be alone with Him. At the time, I had a house full of people because

— PATCHWORK OF PURPOSE —

my daughter was there recovering from surgery, and my two sons were still living at home with us. I got up and got dressed wondering where I was going to end up. As I was contemplating where I could go to sit and be alone with the Lord, I made a quick stop to get a 44oz sweet tea (my most favorite drink) before ending up at the parking lot of our local big chain store. The parking lot was large enough that I could park out of the way and no one would bother me.

As I sat there, I took out my pen and yellow notepad and began writing. God downloaded in me the idea of this book, reminding me of the quilts my mother made for us as we were growing up. He also gave me some of the chapter ideas. As I was writing, my thoughts started to overtake me. *What if no one likes this book? What if it isn't any good? What if I put all this work in and it doesn't make sense? Nobody wants to hear this. No one cares. You are just a small-town girl. You cannot make a difference in anyone else's life.* All these negative thoughts were flooding my mind.

For those of you who do not understand what is happening, the enemy was trying to stop this before I even got started. As I sat there, God showed me those were all lies from the enemy. He showed me His truth just as fast. His word tells us if He started a good work in us, He is faithful enough to complete it. At that very moment, I could see the battle happening. The enemy tells me I am not good enough (like he had my entire life), but God tells me I am His and that is enough. The enemy has me questioning what if no one likes it, reads it, or buys it. God says to me, "What if someone comes to know Me through this?" That is enough for me. The enemy was saying, "How are you going to get this published? You know nothing about that kind of stuff." The enemy was telling me that I could not do this, but God reminded me that He would complete His works.

I do not need to know all the stops. I just have to be faithful to do what God is telling me to do in that moment. In other words, this is His book, this is His work, this is His ideas. I am merely the tool that He was going to use. Over and over, I could hear lies from the enemy but they were instantly followed by God's truth. This lasted a good ten minutes. Talk about having your head and emotions in a spin. It was an awesome encounter with God. He was not going to let the enemy win. What a mighty and faithful God we serve.

The one thing this taught me is the result is not up to me. The result is not up to us. The result belongs to the Lord. The only thing we need to do is be faithful to what He has asked us to do. Take that first step in faith and God will show you the next step. If I had let the enemy win and stopped there, you would not be sitting here reading this book. Just as I have trusted the Lord with this, you can trust Him with whatever task He has set before you. He will use this as part of your testimony moving forward, just as He has done for me.

1. **Romans 1:16**—"For I am not ashamed of the gospel, for it is the power of God for salvation to everyone who believes, to the Jew first and also to the Greek."

2. **1 Peter 3:15**—"But in your hearts honor Christ the Lord as holy, always being prepared to make a defense to anyone who asks you for a reason for the hope that is in you; yet do it with gentleness and respect."

3. **2 Corinthians 5:20**—"Therefore, we are ambassadors for Christ, God making His appeal through us. We implore you on behalf of Christ, be reconciled to God."

4. **Psalm 96:3**—"Declare His glory among the nations, His marvelous works among all the peoples!"

5. **Matthew 28:19-20**—"Go therefore and make disciples of all nations, baptizing them in the name of the Father and of the Son and of the Holy Spirit, teaching them to observe all that I have commanded you. And behold, I am with you always, to the end of the age."

As we transition into Chapter 13, we delve deeper into the significance of each breath we take and the profound meaning behind life's simplest yet most essential moment.

— CHAPTER 13 —
Breath of Life: Finding Meaning in Every Exhale

In this chapter, I am going to talk to you about baby's breath. What do you think of when I say those two words? For some, they will think of the little white flowers that accent larger flowers to make a bouquet fuller and more elegant. Some will think of the actual inhale and exhale of a small child. Either way, you are both correct.

For all you florist and bouquet lovers out there, some would say an arrangement is not complete without the baby's breath. In some cases, you would be correct. In some cases, nothing can be further from the truth. Take the rose for instance. Over the years my husband has sent me several different types of floral arrangements. The classic rose is usually accompanied by baby's breath. No matter if it is one single rose or a dozen. If you call the florist up or order online, most of the time the rose will have baby's breath along with it. Why? Have you seen an arrangement of roses without them? I have and it just seems like something is missing. Do not get me wrong it is still very nice to look at and to smell, but when you add the baby's breath it looks a lot classier and more elegant. The vase is fuller. It is a good accent to the rose.

Now, let's think of the tulip. Every time I have received tulips they are not accompanied by baby's breath. Why? They do not need a filler. It is overkill. The tulip can stand alone. Some may disagree with me on this, but for the sake of my point, I hope you will overlook the difference in opinion on this one thing and continue.

When I hear the words baby's breath it takes on a different meaning. As I sit in the NICU holding my grandson, I can hear every breath. He is on a machine that helps with the pressure and the amount of oxygen he receives with every breath. I sit there and count every breath he takes. As he improves, his doctors are preparing to remove the machine. Adjust this setting. Adjust that setting. He is breathing on his own, he just needs a little help. One day soon, he will no longer need the machine, his body will know what to do to get him what he needs.

> *"The Lord God formed the man from the dust of the ground and breathed into his nostrils the breath of life, and the man became a living being."*
> *— Genesis 2:7*

As I look at both points of view—flower or actual breath—I look for a comparison. Why do they have the same name when one has nothing to do with the other? It does not matter at this point. My point in all this is that God has His hand in both. He has given us many beautiful things that we arrange together. From flower arrangements to decorating our homes, we use fillers and accent pieces. It is all as important as the other, but the actual breath is what I want to concentrate on for a few moments. As I hold this little baby in my arms, knowing he is struggling, there is nothing more precious to me than the sound of his breaths. Why? Because it is proof of life. If you do not have breath, you do not have life.

On one of my visits to the NICU, I was going to hold my grandson. The nurses told us that this is very important for the newborns. So I sat in the designated chair next to his bed and they began to arrange all the cords that were connected to him to make sure they would reach the chair without disconnecting. As they lay him in my arms, I noticed something wasn't right. He was struggling to breathe and the machine alarms were going off. The nurses were all concerned and started to reposition his head and neck as he lay in my arms. It only took a few seconds to realize his lips were turning blue. The tension in the room began to rise. I looked up at the nurse and told her his face was starting to turn blue. They quickly took him from me and laid him back in his bed. They were checking the dials on the computers and things like that. I quickly stood up and moved to the nearest corner of the room to get out of their way. As the alarms on the machine continued to sound, more nurses and a doctor came rushing into the room. They were all checking on him, trying to find out what had happened. The doctor said to them, "Start with the obvious first." I did not know what he was talking about, but as the conversation continued I noticed they were checking all his tubes and wires. Starting with the connection on his body and running the tubes through their hands until they got to the end of it. I heard one nurse say, "He got disconnected." Disconnected? Disconnected from what? The source. The source of his oxygen. As she reconnected him, he began to breathe better and his color started to return to normal.

This really got me thinking. The source. What is our source? What are we connected to? God is our source of everything we need. When we disconnect from God things can go really wrong. The simplicity of this is that as soon as they reconnected him to the oxygen, my grandson started to improve. It did take some time to get him back to where he was, but he eventually got there. That is just like us and God. As soon as we reconnect to Him we start to improve. Sometimes it does take longer than others, but eventually God will get us back to where we were so we can continue to grow in Him.

Sometimes a breath can be the sign of submission. Have you ever had a small child that is fighting his/her sleep? They cry and cry and wiggle and squirm. After what seems like hours they relax, but do not dare lay them down or disturb them because they are not good and sound asleep just yet. So, you sit, and you rock, and you rock until finally there it is. The big sigh. The big inhale. Wait for it, wait for it, and then exhale. The breath. The submission. They could not fight it any longer, so they gave in to what was best for them, and that was rest.

As God looks down on us, He is watching and counting every breath. Is He looking down on us knowing we are struggling? Is He waiting for us to submit to Him? Is He full of joy because we are doing exactly what we are called to do? If you feel you are struggling, what lesson do you think you are meant to learn? God wants us to prosper, but sometimes we must get out of our own way. Sometimes we must get out of His way. He cannot bless us if we are holding onto yesterday. Are you holding onto the flower, the baby's breath? It was only meant to accent you for a time. That season is over. It is beginning to stink up the place. It is no longer beautiful. Stop thinking of the flower and think about the actual breath God just gave you.

> *"But Jesus looked at them and said, 'With man this is impossible, but with God all things are possible.'"*
> — Matthew 19:26

"You are wasting your breath." Have you ever heard that phrase? Have you ever said it? I am guilty on both counts. Most of the time, it means that the person you are trying to get through to is not going to listen. But what if God says to you, "You are wasting your breath"? We only have so many He has allowed us on this planet. What are you doing with yours? Every time you open your mouth to speak, you inhale first: breath. Did you waste your breath? Did you say something negative or uplifting? Did you help someone or hurt them? Was it useless gossip? Wasted breath. We should always have a purpose for our breath. I am working: purpose. I am helping someone: purpose. I am listening: purpose. I am praising God: purpose. I am resting: purpose. Yes. We all need rest. We must be careful that we do not remain at rest over our allotted time. Do not waste your breath.

> *"Let everything that has breath praise the Lord! Praise the Lord!"*
> — Psalm 150:6

In life, we have all been at the place where we feel we cannot catch our breath. Bills are piling up, work is stressful, kids are driving me crazy, school is exhausting, the house needs cleaning, and the yard needs cutting, but I am only

— PATCHWORK OF PURPOSE —

one person. That is when you go to God. He already knows your struggle. He knows you are having trouble catching that breath. He is the machine that has everything you need. He will help you through it. Just connect yourself to Him. It will be a struggle, but there is nothing that He cannot get you through if you surrender the control back to Him. He will adjust the pressure. He will adjust the oxygen level. He will give you everything you need. It will take time, but you will start to feel the effects. He knows what you need. He has what you need. He will give you what you need. All you must do is ask Him. He is waiting for you. His hand is stretched out. Put your hand in His. Speak the words out loud. Admit it to Him. Admit it to yourself. Breathe.

> *"I know what it is to be in need, and I know what it is to have plenty. I have learned the secret of being content in any and every situation, whether well-fed or hungry, whether living in plenty or in want. I can do all things through Him who strengthens me."*
> *— Philippians 4:12-13*

1. **Proverbs 3:5** — "Trust in the Lord with all your heart, and do not lean on your own understanding."

2. **Isaiah 40:31** — "But they who wait for the Lord shall renew their strength; they shall mount up with wings like eagles; they shall run and not be weary; they shall walk and not faint."

3. **Romans 8:28** — "And we know that for those who love God all things work together for good, for those who are called according to His purpose."

4. **Matthew 6:34**—"Therefore do not be anxious about tomorrow, for tomorrow will be anxious for itself. Sufficient for the day is its own trouble."

5. **Joshua 1:9**—"Have I not commanded you? Be strong and courageous. Do not be frightened, and do not be dismayed, for the Lord your God is with you wherever you go."

6. **2 Timothy 3:16**—"All Scripture is breathed out by God and profitable for teaching, for reproof, for correction, and for training in righteousness."

As we conclude our reflection on the breath of life and its significance, we now turn our attention to finding purpose amidst life's messiness. In Chapter 14, we'll explore the beauty of embracing authenticity and compassion, recognizing that our imperfections and struggles are what truly connect us to one another and to our higher calling.

*"Therefore encourage one another
and build one another up, just
as you are doing."*
— 1 Thessalonians 5:11

— CHAPTER 14 —
Finding Purpose in Life's Mess: Embracing Authenticity and Compassion

Have you ever walked through a bookstore and seen the cover of a book that you just had to pick up because it was so appealing? The colors are vibrant, and the words just jump out at you, only for you to open it up and find misspelled words and incomplete sentences. No? I must say this has never happened to me either, but it is a good example of how we see other people and how they see us. Opening this book would be disappointing and why wouldn't it be? It's a mess. Well, welcome to life on planet Earth, it is a mess. We wade through it every day.

So, let us think about it for a minute. You have this person in your life, and they have the perfect book cover. The right car, nice house, the boat, and their yard is always cut (yes there are people out there like that). They have nice clothes and the perfect shoes. They are always happy and always have a smile on their face. I can go on and on. What

— PATCHWORK OF PURPOSE —

you see are coverings. Have you talked to them? Are you worried because you think they have it all together?

"For man looks at the outward appearance, but the Lord looks at the heart."
— 1 Samuel 16:7

I am a firm believer in seasons. People are put in our lives for seasons. It could be a great summer where all you do is have a lot of fun, or maybe they are under the heat of the sun where it seems as if nothing can go right. Maybe it is a long winter where things seem to stay bitter and cold, or the best fall with breathtaking color changes. You will never know what season they are in if you do not interact with them. You could be the ray of hope that God has intended for them. The only way you are going to find out is if you talk to them. A small "hello" and a smile goes a long way.

"A friend loves at all times, and a brother is born for a time of adversity."
— *Proverbs 17:17*

Now you may be thinking that you have nothing to offer them. You have a friendship. You have kindness. You may even have wisdom you do not know about. Above all, you have the love of Christ you can share with them. You have victories, you have valleys. It may help them to know you have gone through the exact situation they are in and God pulled you out. They may need someone to just sit and listen for a while.

"Whoever brings blessing will be enriched, and one who waters will himself be watered."
— *Proverbs 11:25*

— TESSICA DAVIS —

Let me tell you a quick story. I have a friend just like that. She is beautiful, kind, honest, generous, and genuine. She has a nice car, a great house, a pool in the backyard, and a great family. I can go on and on about her. She is awesome. She always has that beautiful smile on her face. To someone on the outside looking in, you would think she has the perfect life and nothing ever goes wrong. Even with all that, each time we sit and talk about serious topics, she shares with me the struggles she is going through. (We all have them.) After a long conversation, and me sharing what God has put on my heart to share, she often tells me that she needed to hear this or that. Depending on what I had to say about whatever situation she was going through at the time. There was something going on in her life that I was able to shed light on or just give her confirmation that she was following God's Will in her life. And guess what? I did not even know what she was praying about beforehand. She has her own struggles just like everyone else. Being open to the Holy Spirit when speaking with others is a gift. You have to get out of your own head, out of your fleshly emotions, and look at the situation as God does. We have to be careful that we do not give the advice our flesh and emotions would offer, that is where we can go wrong. We do not want to lead someone further down the wrong path, but gently bring them back to what the Word of God says about the situation.

> *"Bear one another's burdens,*
> *and so fulfill the law of Christ."*
> *— Galatians 6:2*

How many of you would agree with me if I said life is messy? Every day brings its own challenges to pile on top of yesterday's. Some days we overcome a challenge or solve a problem just to have one, two, or eight come along. The point of asking my question is to propose a different outlook. Some days I wake up with the question, "What will today bring me?" That is not a bad question. It's all about perspective and the way the question is meant.

Did I mean what problem am I going to have that I cannot fix? Did I mean what bill did I forget to pay knowing the money is not yet in the bank? Is it that I have the feeling that I will meet people I do not particularly like or care to be around? All these come to mind from time to time.

Let us look at this question from a different angle. What will today bring me? Where can I look to find joy? Can I take pride in helping those around me? What will I learn today? How can I grow? It is all from the same question but with a different perspective. This is not to say the other will not come. But why search them out?

"Rejoice always, pray continually,
give thanks in all circumstances; for
this is God's will for you in Christ Jesus."
— *1 Thessalonians 5:16-18*

Oh, how I love that word, perspective. I like to study and learn about perspective. Glass half empty or glass half full kind of stuff. Over the years I have noticed as we go through our day, we meet a variety of people. We meet people we know at work, school, the gym, and we meet other people we do not know at the grocery store, coffee shop, convenience store, or any place we happen to find ourselves that day. As we greet with Southern hospitality, we often say something like, "Good morning," "Good afternoon," or "How are you?" Mostly out of habit. The most common answer is the "Good morning/afternoon, I am fine," or "All is well." type of reply. However, if we were being honest, we would have to say, "I am worried because my child is sick," "I am sad or depressed because I just lost a friend," "I could not sleep last night due to stress over bills or home repairs that are needed," or "Everything in life seems to be going wrong, I don't think life is worth living." We as people like to just give the polite answer and keep going. I have found myself guilty of that very thing. My friends will ask how I am doing and instead of telling the truth, I give the polite answer. I thank God that He has put people in my life that will call me out on it. They tell me, "Okay, that is the polite answer, but I can see something is wrong. Share with me." Sometimes we cry together. Sometimes we pray together. Sometimes they have a word from God about the situation.

I had a friend who each time anyone would ask him the question, "How are you?" or "How is it going?" the answer was always the same: "Fantastic." He would even draw the word out, making it a lot longer than just a quick answer. But like I said, he and his wife were my friends, so I knew he had issues at home that he was dealing with, just like everyone else. The purpose of his answer escaped me for years. Was he being sarcastic? Was he just giving the polite answer in his own way? Did he really not want to talk about it? I would just shrug it off and go about my day. Now that I think about it, I believe I understand. He was looking for the fantastic in every day. How would your life change if you looked for positivity all day? A lot of the times we focus on what is going wrong instead of what is going right. Even the work of God tells us to focus on what is going well in our lives. I am not saying to ignore all the bad things, just don't give them your main focus.

— PATCHWORK OF PURPOSE —

"Finally, brothers and sisters, whatever is true, whatever is noble, whatever is right, whatever is pure, whatever is lovely, whatever is admirable—if anything is excellent or praiseworthy—think about such things."
— Philippians 4:8

The Bible tells us, "Seek and ye shall find" (Matthew 7:7). We must be careful what we are seeking. This works for the bad as well as for the good. If we meditate on all the struggles we face, or what potential struggles will come, then we are seeking them out. Being prepared is one thing, but what are your expectations? I have caught myself saying in frustration, "Well I knew that would happen." Not that I am all-knowing or anything, but that is what I expected, so that is what I got. We do not intentionally look or wish for negative things to enter our lives, but we must be mindful of what comes out of our mouths. Guard your thoughts because if you are anything like me, whatever you are thinking will come out of your mouth. This is something I had to learn the hard way. Speak life in the situation. Speak the answer you have been praying for.

"Set a guard, O Lord, over my mouth; keep watch over the door of my lips!"
— Psalm 141:3

Looking back on my life, I can see I have overcome several things that could potentially help those around me, but because I want to appear that I have it all together, I do not always share my problems, concerns, or my victories. It has been revealed to me that I am doing an injustice to many by not sharing. Sometimes it gives people hope from knowing someone else is dealing with some of the same things they are. Maybe they can find some hope or some comfort knowing someone else has been where they are. Hopefully, they can find the confidence and the strength to keep going knowing they are not alone.

> *"Therefore encourage one another and build one another up, just as you are doing."*
> *— 1 Thessalonians 5:11*

My point is this: You DO have something to offer this world. You DO have a purpose. You ARE enough. You ARE a blessing. You ARE an inspiration. Sometimes you are all these things to others without realizing it.

You do the best you can do each day with God's guidance and know that God is using the seeds you plant in the lives of others as well as in your own. You may not be present for their harvest. Maybe that is not the season you were meant to experience. Do not go through life wanting what someone else has, all you see is the covering. Instead, help them through their winter. You are what they need in their life right now. Spring will come for you in time. Go out and be a blessing to those around you.

> *"Each of you should use whatever gift you have received to serve others, as faithful stewards of God's grace in its various forms."*
> *— 1 Peter 4:10*

We all have things we can share to help those around us. Be the kind voice someone needs to hear. Be that smile to those around you. Your kindness can be as small as a handshake, a hug, a smile, or a compliment. You do not know the whole story just by looking at the cover of someone else's book. Go and look for the fantastic in every day and

— PATCHWORK OF PURPOSE —

help those around you do the same. Invite them for coffee or lunch. Sit down with them and take some time to show them they are cared for; you never know what God has in store for them. He may even use the situation to bring some clarity to some things in your own life. I often find that when I step out in faith and spend time with someone new, God blesses me just as much as He does them in that moment. Sometimes it is a new revelation and sometimes it is a new bond with a new friend.

> *"Let us not become weary in doing good,*
> *for at the proper time we will reap a*
> *harvest if we do not give up."*
> *— Galatians 6:9*

1. **Philippians 4:6** — "Do not be anxious about anything, but in every situation, by prayer and petition, with thanksgiving, present your requests to God."

2. **Romans 8:28** — "And we know that in all things God works for the good of those who love Him, who have been called according to His purpose."

3. **Isaiah 40:31** — "But those who hope in the Lord will renew their strength. They will soar on wings like eagles; they will run and not grow weary, they will walk and not be faint."

4. **Proverbs 3:5-6** — "Trust in the Lord with all your heart and lean not on your own understanding; in all your ways submit to Him, and He will make your paths straight."

5. **Jeremiah 29:11**—"'For I know the plans I have for you,' declares the Lord, 'plans to prosper you and not to harm you, plans to give you hope and a future.''

As we embrace the authenticity of our own journeys and extend compassion to others, we embark on a path of self-discovery and growth. Chapter 14 illuminated the beauty found in life's messiness and the importance of being genuine in our interactions. Now, in Chapter 15, we delve into the transformative power of forgiveness, understanding, and grace. These virtues not only heal wounds but also pave the way for deeper connections and a more meaningful existence.

"Let us not become weary in doing good, for at the proper time we will reap a harvest if we do not give up."
— *Galatians 6:9*

CHAPTER 15
Shining Light: Spreading Joy and Love in Everyday Moments

It is a beautiful day! Sun is shining. Birds are chirping. The wind is blowing. Oh, wait I forgot, it is July here in Texas and it is HOT! What does that mean? Nothing...your day is what you make of it. Be the wind. Be the brightness or the bird's song around you.

> *"Light is sweet, and it pleases the eyes to see the sun."*
> — Ecclesiastes 11:7

Hum a tune to an old sitcom and make people around you wonder, "Where did I hear that before?" Wave at a neighbor. Ask a silly question without expecting an answer. Smile at a stranger. The smallest things you do could make a huge impact on those around you.

— PATCHWORK OF PURPOSE —

*"A cheerful heart is good medicine, but
a crushed spirit dries up the bones."*
— Proverbs 17:22

Adding simple acts of kindness and joy can significantly impact the people around you. Even small gestures like smiling or waving can brighten someone's day. This aligns with biblical principles of spreading joy and kindness.

You may be the only smiling face they see all day. Tell a lame joke. People around you may roll their eyes at you. Guess what, you made an impression. Sometime later that day, some of those same people will say, "Oh. I remember that tune," or they may secretly laugh at the joke that is now stuck in their head. They may finally discover the answer and it give them a small sense of satisfaction.

*"A cheerful look brings joy to the heart;
good news makes for good health."*
— Proverbs 15:30

Even if the impact isn't immediately visible, small acts of positivity can linger in people's minds, bringing moments of joy later on. This aligns with the biblical teaching of sowing seeds of joy and laughter.

Some of the people I worked with came to expect me to start our conversations with a funny story. As they walked up to me, or I to them, I would do the customary, "Hello. Good morning. How are you?" type of thing and then I would just extend both my arms towards them and just say, "Funny Story..." at that point I would just continue with whatever short story I would have for the day.

— TESSICA DAVIS —

*"Anxiety weighs down the heart,
but a kind word cheers it up."*
— Proverbs 12:25

Creating a positive atmosphere through humor and light-heartedness can alleviate stress and create a more enjoyable work environment, reflecting the importance of uplifting others. My stories were usually something silly one of my kids had done or said. Or something I did that was way out of character like forgetting something that should have been second nature. Maybe something I forgot to do. Or an exit I missed and ended up way away from my destination before I discovered the mistake. Over time, I found out that these little funny stories were the highlight of their day. Working in a high-stress position, sometimes you need a break in the day. And what better way to reduce stress than with a funny story or a lame joke?

*"A happy heart makes the face cheerful,
but heartache crushes the spirit."*
— Proverbs 15:13

Sharing personal anecdotes can humanize the workplace environment and provide much-needed moments of levity, reinforcing the importance of maintaining joy even in challenging circumstances.

Funny story: My son Jordan came home on his lunch break with his "to go" bag from the local burrito and taco stand in hand. He sat down and started eating and said out of the blue, "Cheese makes everything better." I just looked at him and said "Okay," with a little laugh. He said, "Think about it. What hot food wouldn't taste better with cheese on top?" with a little laugh.

— PATCHWORK OF PURPOSE —

This boy is serious about his cheese. I started thinking. I could not come up with anything, so we just sat in silence as he continued to eat. After about thirty minutes, I broke the silence with "Hot apple pie." Jordan just busted out laughing and exclaimed, "You've been sitting there thinking about that this whole time?" Then we both had a good long laugh. He had finished his lunch and needed to get ready to return to work so he stood up and started to pack up his "to go" bag and all his wrappers.

My son, a lot like his mom, likes to have the last word so he replied, "Cream cheese. You can put cream cheese on hot apple pie." Like I said, he is serious about his cheese. If you like cream cheese on hot apple pie, or not is irrelevant. The point is: He made me think. He made me laugh.

Now, this had no impact on anything I did that day…or did it? I still laugh about it even today, several years later. He brightened my day. No money was spent. No real effort was made, other than a conversation. A silly conversation that made me think. How much change can you make around you by being that light or having that silly conversation? Make someone laugh. Make them think. Let yourself laugh. Sometimes you need to laugh at yourself.

"All the days of the oppressed are wretched, but the cheerful heart has a continual feast."
— Proverbs 15:15

If nothing else people think you are crazy. Sometimes at work, sitting at my desk I would often remember little things like my story about Jordan and his cheese and let out a little chuckle. My co-workers started inquiring, "What was so funny?" They would ask over and over until I shared the story. I often got a laugh out of them. Sometimes I got a glimpse of their eye roll, or they may even offer an "ugh" in disgust because my story did not offer up the latest juicy gossip. However their reply and whatever they thought had no merit, it made my day better. Sometimes it was just the laugh one of them needed to get through the day.

> *"A cheerful look brings joy to the heart;*
> *good news makes for good health."*
> *— Proverbs 15:30*

As far as the eye rolls and the "ugh" you may encounter, the only advice I can offer is to let haters hate. Just because someone is not receptive at that moment, does not mean it will not help them later. They could be going through something that is weighing heavy on them. Do not let them get you down. You do not have to let it get confrontational. Just be yourself. Sometimes we have to just let it roll off our backs. Laugh anyway. Sing the song. Tell the story. Spread the joy and the laughter.

> *"But I tell you, love your enemies*
> *and pray for those who persecute you."*
> *— Matthew 5:44*

All of this to say, be the best you that you can be. Make sure your days are filled with all God has for you. We do not have to seek out those who will not like it, they will be there. Just let God's light shine through. At the end of your life, and as much as we don't like talking about your earthly life ending, what will your loved ones remember the most? Is it your love and compassion? Is it you sitting up with them when they were hurting? Is it your silliness? Is it all those funny stories and lame jokes? Is it the fact that you had a way of making even a heavy situation feel lighter after talking with you? Is what they remember most going to be a beautiful memory or is it bad memories that could potentially lead them to making bad choices of their own?

> *"Let us not become weary in doing good,*
> *for at the proper time we will reap*
> *a harvest if we do not give up."*
> — Galatians 6:9

The legacy one leaves behind underscores the importance of living a life filled with love, compassion, and joy, aligning with the biblical call to lead a life of righteousness and kindness.

I have people in my life with whom most of my memories are not warm, welcoming, or even wanted if I am being honest. These people made things harder on me and those around me. They were always negative or even nasty-tempered. Even the air felt heavy when they were around. They did not understand the full impact they were making as they were going through their days. So with that being said, what are you leaving behind? Is it negativity, judgment, and condemnation, or is joy, cheerfulness, truth in love, and understanding?

> *"Be kind and compassionate to*
> *one another, forgiving each other,*
> *just as in Christ God forgave you."*
> — Ephesians 4:32

As we talked about in the first chapter, every choice we make, every action we take is recorded. Even those little things we think are done in secret will all come to light eventually. What patterns are you making today? What type of fabric are you creating?

> *"But I tell you that everyone will have to give account on the day of judgment for every empty word they have spoken."*
> — Matthew 12:36

Recognizing the accountability for our actions emphasizes the importance of living a life of integrity and righteousness. My wish is that at the end of my earthly journey my life quilt is full of vibrant, fun, and bright colors. There will be bad choices, rough days, mistakes, and even sadness mixed in, but overall my wish is that my family and friends can be wrapped and kept warm in the memories I have left behind with them. I keep this at the forefront of my mind. Are they seeing God in me? Am I showing them the love of Jesus each time they come in contact with me?

Aspiring to leave behind a legacy of love and joy lined with the teachings of God's word is what I choose to focus on. God's promise of eternal joy and fulfillment in the presence of God, emphasizes the importance of living a life that reflects His love and grace.

I hope this has helped you look at your life and your daily choices a little differently. I pray that every person that reads or even touches this book will know Jesus Christ as Lord and Saviour and you will have a meaningful life and a full relationship with Him. I hope to be standing in heaven with you praising our Lord together. Until then, please remember YOU HAVE A PURPOSE FOR BEING HERE. Much love and God bless you with love, laughter, and a lifetime of happiness.

— PATCHWORK OF PURPOSE —

"And the peace of God, which transcends all understanding, will guard your hearts and your minds in Christ Jesus."
— Philippians 4:7

1. **Romans 12:15** — "Rejoice with those who rejoice; mourn with those who mourn."

2. **Proverbs 15:13** — "A happy heart makes the face cheerful, but heartache crushes the spirit."

3. **Colossians 3:17** — "And whatever you do, whether in word or deed, do it all in the name of the Lord Jesus, giving thanks to God the Father through Him."

4. **Philippians 2:4** — "Let each of you look not only to his own interests but also to the interests of others."

5. **Galatians 6:2** — "Carry each other's burdens, and in this way you will fulfill the law of Christ."

As we reflect on the lessons explored in Chapter 15, we recognize the transformative impact these principles have on our lives. They serve as the cornerstone of our journey toward fulfillment and purpose. Now, in our concluding chapter, we consolidate our insights, reaffirm our commitments, and celebrate the richness of our experiences. Join me as we bid farewell to this chapter of our lives and embrace the new beginnings that await us up ahead.

— CONCLUSION —
Threads of Legacy

As I sit here reflecting back on the journey we've taken together through the pages of this book, I am reminded of the patchwork quilt that adorned my childhood home. Each scrap of fabric, meticulously stitched together by my mother's loving hands, created a masterpiece of warmth and comfort. In much the same way, our lives are a tapestry woven from the threads of our daily choices, each decision carefully intertwined by the hand of God.

Just as my mother's quilt provided solace on cold nights, so too should our legacy offer warmth and comfort to the generations that follow. It is a testament to the love and dedication we pour into the lives of others, leaving behind a legacy that transcends time.

My mother, a beacon of faith and devotion, instilled in me the importance of spiritual grounding. She faithfully led our family to church, never wavering in her commitment to nurturing our souls. It was in those moments, kneeling together at our living room sofa, that she imparted the greatest gift of all: a relationship with Christ. It is my most treasured memory, kneeling next to her in that old house as she helped lead me to the Lord in prayer. What a pivotal moment as our legacies intertwined. Thank you, Lord.

— PATCHWORK OF PURPOSE —

Though I may have strayed from the path at times, the wisdom of Scripture rings true: "Train up a child in the way he should go: and when he is old, he will not depart from it" (Proverbs 22:6). Just as my mother's teachings shaped my faith, so too will this book serve as a cornerstone for the legacy I leave behind.

As we turn the final page of this journey, let us embrace the profound truth that our lives are but a small part of a much grander story, one that continues to unfold with each passing day. May our legacy be a testament to the love, grace, and compassion we have shown to others, and may it serve as a guiding light for generations to come.

With grateful hearts and hopeful spirits, let us step boldly into the future, knowing that our legacy will endure long after we are gone. For in the end, it is not the wealth or possessions we leave behind that truly matter, but the impact we have had on the lives of those around us. And so, with faith as our compass and love as our guide, let us write the next chapter of our legacy with purpose and intention.

1. **Building a Legacy:**

    - "But lay up for yourselves treasures in heaven, where neither moth nor rust destroys and where thieves do not break in and steal." (Matthew 6:20)

    - "And whatever you do, whether in word or deed, do it all in the name of the Lord Jesus, giving thanks to God the Father through Him." (Colossians 3:17)

2. **Inviting Jesus into Your Life:**

    - "Yet to all who did receive Him, to those who believed in His name, He gave the right to become children of God." (John 1:12)

    - "Behold, I stand at the door and knock. If anyone hears My voice and opens the door, I will come in to him and eat with him, and he with Me." (Revelation 3:20)

3. **Maintaining Faith and Trust:**

    - "Trust in the Lord with all your heart, and do not lean on your own understanding. In all your ways acknowledge Him, and He will make straight your paths." (Proverbs 3:5-6)

    - "And we know that in all things God works for the good of those who love Him, who have been called according to His purpose." (Romans 8:28)

4. **Accepting God's Plans and Changes:**

    - "For I know the plans I have for you, declares the Lord, plans for welfare and not for evil, to give you a future and a hope." (Jeremiah 29:11)

    - "For My thoughts are not your thoughts, neither are your ways My ways, declares the Lord." (Isaiah 55:8)

— PATCHWORK OF PURPOSE —

5. **Perseverance and Endurance:**

    - "Blessed is the man who remains steadfast under trial, for when he has stood the test he will receive the crown of life, which God has promised to those who love Him." (James 1:12)

    - "I can do all things through Him who strengthens me." (Philippians 4:13)

6. **Living a Purposeful Life:**

    - "Let your light shine before others, so that they may see your good works and give glory to your Father who is in heaven." (Matthew 5:16)

    - "And let us not grow weary of doing good, for in due season we will reap, if we do not give up." (Galatians 6:9)

Words of Encouragement from the Author

I hope this has helped you look at your life and your choices a little differently. I pray that you (and every person who reads or even touches this book) will know Jesus Christ as your personal Lord and Savoir. I pray you have a meaningful life and a full relationship with Him. I hope to one day be standing in heaven with you praising our Lord together. Until then, please remember YOU HAVE A PURPOSE FOR BEING HERE.

*May The Lord bless you and keep you;
May the Lord make His face shine on you and
be gracious to you; May the Lord turn His face
toward you and give you peace.
— Numbers 6:24*

Special Thanks

Special thanks to God on high. Hallelujah! I give you all the praise, honor, and glory.

I want to personally thank all my friends and family, as well as my extended friends and family, for their incredible support during this journey. The overwhelming amount of financial blessings, prayers, encouragement, and love has deeply touched my heart. I will be forever grateful and will never forget your kindness. This achievement would not have been possible without you. I pray for God's blessings to fall like rain upon each one of you. I love you all.

I give all my praise and worship to God. May He alone have all the glory.